For Geo,
My favorite sister-in-
law and golf partner,
We had lots of fun
times at Mountain
Shadows on
Sunday.
Love,
Annie

**Other titles by the author:
As One Door Closes
Reinvented Lives**

Sex and the Single Senior

by

Annie Weissman

Scottsdale Press

Chapter One
Player Number One

How to start dating? I couldn't see me doing the bar scene. My middle son, twenty-three-years old, partied there. I don't like golf or poker. My sister suggested jdate.com, a Jewish dating service. My Phoenix friends laughed when they heard I was considering joining because although I'm Jewish, I'd hardly ever dated Jewish guys in my life. My rationale was that the Jewish community in Phoenix was small, so jdate seemed less intimidating than Match.com, which had many more members. That would come later when I built up my confidence.

One night, when my youngest son, fourteen, was staying at a friend's house so I had privacy, I signed up and filled out the profile, then called my best friend Susan to approve it. I was unsure about the part where I wrote, "I'm fifty-five and not embarrassed to say it. I'm a semi-retired educator who still teaches on the college level and writes books. I love swimming in the ocean, Suns games, movies, laughter, and optimism. I'm looking for some great, but safe, sex."

"I just read a review about *A Round-Heeled Woman: My Late Life Adventures in Sex and Romance* by Jane Juska. She had placed a personal ad in *The New York Review of Books*, saying she wanted great sex before her sixtieth birthday. Jane met and had sex with many men, some kind, some not."

"Leave the statement in," Susan said. "Which photo are you going to use?"

"The one I had my neighbor snap for a speaking brochure," I said.

"Oh no!" Susan said. "You should use the glamour shot that was on the back cover of your last book."

"Okay. It looks enough like me so a guy wouldn't feel fooled."

I paid the fee via credit card and waited for something to happen. My "matches" finally arrived. I perused the twenty profiles carefully, as if examining bacteria in a petri dish. I emailed ten of them. And waited. I finally went to sleep.

*   *
*

By the next morning I got mail from Jdate. I logged in and looked up the reply. It was from a guy who was five foot seven. I'm five nine. I figured since I was a grownup and not looking for Mr. Perfect, I didn't care about height, so I emailed him back. He emailed me his phone number and I called. We had a fun conversation. He was obviously interested in the sexual comment I made.

I was horny as all get out, so I joked along. We made a date for dinner the next night. He asked how he would recognize me. I told him I looked just like my photo except my hair was styled a little differently and would be wearing the same purple scarf that I did in my profile photo.

I went to the drug store and discreetly searched for the section with condoms. STDs were rampant among my age group. Since I'd had the tests for them all, including AIDS, when I divorced my cheating husband, I knew I was clear—still clear since I hadn't had sex since then.

I found the section and was dumbfounded at the large selection. I'd never had to worry about this before. The last time I was single between marriages, it was before AIDS and after my hysterectomy, so I couldn't get pregnant. Foolish me, I wasn't thinking about other STDs at that time.

Would I insult a guy if I got medium-sized condoms? Did all men think they were large-sized? Did I want lubricated or ribbed? I took estrogen, notwithstanding the new research, so I didn't need lubrication. Was the ribbing for me or for him? I decided to purchase the ribbed ones and find out. And I bought the large size.

I took my time deciding what to wear for the date. When it's 110 degrees in Phoenix, the choices narrow. You know the old saying, the difference between a married woman and a single one is fifteen pounds? In my case, I'd taken off thirty-five to make myself comfortable, though I was still "full figured." I wore a Chico's outfit to look the thinnest— black Travelers pants; a purple tank top; and a black Travelers collared jacket, with the purple scarf placed carefully to look casual.

I started out early but had trouble finding the restaurant, having to stop at two fast-food restaurants to pee. It happens when I'm nervous. I was on time, but my date was already there waiting. His appearance did not correspond with his picture. The guy, Player Number One in the profile, had a big hunk of black hair. The man before me had gray hair that was getting sparse. He was stocky, thank goodness. I wouldn't crush him in the heat of passion.

Hmm, guess there's no truth in dating even though he had written under *Ideal Relationship* that he wanted "total honesty and disclosure. There should be no secrets or surprises."

The dinner conversation wasn't as forced as I had feared, though he did keep asking questions like, "Am I the first guy you've been out with?" and "Are you dating any other guys from Jdate?" I learned that he was an accountant/financial consultant and he had grown children.

After dinner I followed in my car to his apartment. It was a mess. I guess he didn't care about first impressions.

He put on some music and we sat on the floor on cushions—so sixties. He kissed me, and I welcomed it. It'd been far too long since someone had kissed me. He nibbled on my ear. I was ready to tear his clothes off. But then he would take *my* clothes off. I hadn't been naked in front of a guy other than my husband for seventeen years, and it was still light outside.

We kissed some more, and I could feel my sexual urge, repressed for seventeen months, roar back to life. I kissed him back passionately.

He suggested we go into the bedroom. When I took off my bra, his eyes went wild, and his head bobbed up and down. He said he'd never seen real breasts that large in person. I finally got naked and slid under the sheet. Should I have grabbed the condoms from my purse before getting into bed?

He barely touched me, and I was off on an orgasm, laughing my head off. The laughing part was disconcerting to him. I had explained beforehand that some women are screamers, but I was a giggler and laugher.

His "throbbing member" was short, like him, but it appeared fat enough to do the job. He reached into his night stand, pulled out a condom, and put it on.

"Here," he said. "Put this on me."

He handed me something on him that looked like a cheap napkin ring.

"What is it?" I asked.

"It's a cock ring to keep me hard," he said.

I guess the sexual performance concerns of male baby boomers are different now than twenty years ago.

Now I know why society tells us to date men our height or taller. Or maybe it was just him. It was tough to find a position that worked. I felt like a pancake being flipped.

"What do you want me to do for you?" he asked.

"You already did," I answered. "That was what the giggling was about."

"Ah, I guess that makes us Body Buddies."

He came, I guess. I couldn't really feel it. His "member" stayed up. I was not a complete ignoramus about sex. From experience, I knew that men deflate after ejaculation. Some get aroused again soon, and some must be coaxed. I'd never seen anyone stay hard. Then it hit me. Viagra.

I stifled a yawn, ready to go home, but he obviously wanted more. I did him the courtesy but stifled a yawn. When he called me "Big Momma" and told me I was the first "big" woman he ever had sex with, I was insulted. How dare he comment on my weight.

Why didn't I say so? I'm normally an assertive person. I wanted honesty, but not tactless honesty. Maybe it had to do with having all my clothes off in a stranger's apartment.

Before I left, he gave me the advice to drink plenty of cranberry juice, so I wouldn't get a urinary tract infection, as happens sometimes if one hasn't had sex for a while. He called after I got home to make sure I arrived safely. That was considerate. Maybe he was okay. Or was I desperate?

He called the next day. After some small talk, he said, "Are you free tonight?"

"Yeah, what do you have in mind?"

"Nothing in particular."

"How about going to a club to listen to music?"

"I'm tired. How about we meet me at my apartment?"

I glared at the phone, then made excuses and hung up.

The more I thought about it, the angrier I got. We both wanted "body buddies," but we had different accents on the phrase. I wanted a body BUDDY with whom to hang out and have sex, and he wanted a BODY buddy with the emphasis on easy sex. There would be no second date.

Maybe if he'd been better in bed, I might have given him another chance, though he didn't deserve it. I called him and told him that it didn't work for me and we wouldn't go out again. That felt right. I was embarrassed by the urgency of my sexual needs but next time would be different. Something about this encounter didn't feel right. Maybe it was the messy apartment—a metaphor that I didn't merit enough of his respect to spruce up the place.

Lesson learned: Avoid men who don't put the emphasis on the right word for Body Buddies.

Chapter Two

The Casanova

A month later I decided to try jdate again. I emailed all the matches I'd received in the past month—Russ, Bruce, Beal, Mark, John, Bert, Gipper, David, Alaska, 818, Good Catch, Featherinmycap, Bunky, and Phoenix Man.

I received some replies, but the one I was most interested in was Phoenix Man. He was a sixty-two-year-old nonsmoker, five foot eleven, carried a few extra pounds, and he was looking for a date, a friend, a long-term relationship. The only negative was that he was a right-wing moderate; I'm a flaming liberal. His profile said his perfect match was "a single, Jewish, professional woman in the Phoenix area, who is interested in a casual dating relationship. She can be average in all regards except intelligence, in which I would prefer that she be well above average."

His profile said this about his ideal relationship: "I am interested in a dating relationship for companionship . . . theater, movies, sporting events. A long-term relationship is possible, but not marriage."

Hmmm, I was a Phoenix Suns season-ticket holder. Maybe this was someone to enjoy the rest of the season with.

I wrote, *"It's so nice to read in a dating profile that intelligence is valued. I am intelligent but not egotistical. I love to laugh. If you're interested, email me."*

He emailed me the next day: *Hi Annie, Not that I'm Einstein either. . . But if I am going to spend time with someone, I must be able to talk with her. I have found over the years that for me, regardless of what else there is going for it, an I.Q. of room temperature makes for a short relationship. I will be out of town for a while on business. If you want to email me, please use my business e-mail address.*
Casanova

We emailed, and then called each other. He was in Chicago; I was at home, then on a beach vacation in California with my family and friends. In our phone conversations, Casanova lived up to his profile. We discussed the no-no's: politics and religion. Then we chatted about current events and the books we were reading. Was this too good to be true?

He called at eight on a Tuesday night in August about two weeks after we started emailing and told me he was on his way home from the airport and wanted to meet me for a cup of coffee. Since he hadn't included a picture in his profile, I told him I would wear a purple blouse. We agreed to meet at a Starbucks in north Phoenix at a remote outdoor mall. This was quite far from my home in central Phoenix.

I had just enough time to take a shower, put on some eye makeup, but not enough time to agonize over what to wear. It took only twenty minutes to get there as the freeway was devoid of traffic. Even so, I was late because I had a hard time finding the Starbucks.

I finally called him. "I can't find the Starbucks."

He laughed. "Where are you/"

"By the movie theater"

He laughed again. "Don't move. I'll meet you there."

Casanova seemed younger than sixty-two. He'd been honest about his height, but I didn't see any extra pounds. He was balding, with reddish brown hair, a well-groomed but full moustache, and glasses. He was wearing a pair of slacks and a black tee shirt. I liked the package.

At Starbucks I ordered an iced tea but didn't buy my own drink as he took out his wallet and paid before I had time to open my purse. We sat in comfy armchairs for a long time chatting about his work, my work, his children, my children, and news of the day. We both made sure to insert into the conversation that we didn't want to marry.

Casanova had lied a little in his profile, though I'm not sure what difference two years makes. He was only sixty, and he lived in north Scottsdale. When I asked why he lied, he said he hadn't wanted to attract someone looking for money. Then he suggested we take a walk. We strolled around, listened to some bands that were showing their stuff, and stopped to browse at a bookstore.

After an hour, I was boiling up. In August in Phoenix it's still over a hundred degrees at ten at night. I wasn't about to be perceived as a weenie, so I forged ahead. Plus, I didn't want to leave this guy. There are times in life with both men and women that two people click as friends, daters, lovers. I didn't know which he would be, but he was someone I wanted to know better.

I asked him to accompany me to a Phoenix Mercury basketball game a few days later. I had season tickets for both the men's team, the Suns, and the women's team, the Mercury. Since I believe in supporting women's sports, I've had tickets for many seasons. My seats were only twelve dollars each, but they're in the eighth row. I was impressed that he didn't balk at attending a women's basketball game.

We had a great time cheering and yelling. Instead of going home after the game, he suggested a blues bar near downtown called Char's Has the Blues. It's a funky venue crowded with tables and a long polished wooden bar. We sat at a table in the back and listened to the band, drank beers, and played with each other's arms. He rubbed my back and the electricity flowed from there. We kissed when he left me at my door.

      *   *   *   *

      *

We made a date to have dinner on Saturday night. I drove to his home since the restaurant was in his ritzy section of Scottsdale, about twenty-five miles from my place. I was still holding to the safety rule of having my own escape. His impressive home was in an exclusive development. He gave me a house tour.

"Who was your decorator?" I asked.

He skewed his mouth to the side, not pleased by my observation. "What do you mean?"

"Nothing, really. It just looks too perfect to be designed by a mortal man."

He nodded. "I bought the model home with all the furnishings.

That made sense. He was an engineer and could afford it. Everything was in its place and the throw cushions on the sofa were in perfect alignment.

He took me to a steak restaurant that I'd been to before—very chic, very expensive, very tasty, and reportedly owned by the Mafia. The décor was black leather booths and dim lighting. Garlic wafted up to tickle my nose. He talked about his late wife, whom he obviously loved. He also mentioned that he had just changed the status of a four-year relationship. It had been exclusive, but the woman decided she wanted to marry. Casanova didn't. Sounded good to me.

When I finally put my fork down, a thought came to me. *Should offer to pay? Ask him.*

"Could I pay for my dinner?"

He smiled "I'm glad you asked. I would have been insulted if you'd pulled out cash or a credit card."

I started to object, but he interrupted me.

"Let's strike a bargain. I hate to plan activities. You plan our dates and I'll pay for them. Deal?"

So there'd be more dates. I wasn't totally comfortable with the arrangement, but I decided to see how long I dated him before bringing it up again.

After dinner, we returned to his home. I had mentioned that my back was hurting, and he offered to give me a back rub. We went into his bedroom and I lay down on the bed. We kissed for a long time. I felt the sexual urge, but suppressed it in favor of the romantic necking.

After a while he whispered in my ear, "I'm going to get some lotion. Why don't you . . . get more comfortable . . . so I can massage your back?"

I complied but knew I was not going to bed with him that night. It was too soon, and he didn't press me. He gave me a fabulous back rub. Afterwards I got up, got dressed, and went home. I felt valued, appreciated, and desirable.

We developed a routine of going out to dinner, then enjoyed live music at the Rhythm Room or Char's Has the Blues, or went to a play. Our discussions were intellectual and fantastic, and we even played Scrabble. He listened to what I said and took it seriously because he knew I was intelligent and well informed.

Casanova liked the fact that I had a better vocabulary than he did. One day, he used "hegemony" correctly, but I didn't know what it meant. He was thrilled to explain to me that "hegemony" was a state of having influence over another. We enjoyed discovering something the other knew nothing about. He taught me about "cargo cultists," and I taught him about American "orphan trains." We lent and bought each other books.

However, this was a "limited" relationship for several reasons:

- He worked at least half the month in Chicago.
- He had another woman, F, in Phoenix he dated. He had been exclusive with her until she wanted marriage.
- He hated holidays, and I loved them. We never spent them with each other.
- We always went to his place because he hated dogs—I had three—and I didn't want to get my son involved with my dates.

At the beginning, I was jealous yet a little intrigued with being the "other woman," as F didn't know about me. But then I realized that the relationship was beneficial to me in important ways:

- I had someone of the opposite sex who enjoyed my company.

19

- He paid for his ticket ($65) when we went to Phoenix Suns games.
- I was guaranteed great sex a few times a month with someone I cared for without the hassle of "finding" someone.
- He didn't care about my weight. He always called me "pretty lady" and complimented me on my body. (Maybe that should have been #1.)
- I enjoyed his company and our intellectual connection.
- I didn't have to talk to him every day or worry about what he thought or include him in my life or spend a lot of mental or physical time with him.

I used to be a jealous person, probably fueled by the fact that both of my husbands cheated on me, but I wasn't jealous with Casanova. He wasn't the perfect guy, but the relationship met my needs. Was that why? I realized I had a sixties attitude about him that reminded me of open marriages.

One night, we were at an Italian restaurant at the Esplanade I'd found in the

Arizona Republic's "Best of Phoenix" supplement. We waited a while for a table as the restaurant didn't take reservations for parties fewer than six.

During dinner, our spirited-but-not-accusatory conversation centered on conservative and liberal commentators. I was reading the new Al Franken book, and he was reading the Ann Coulter one about liberals being traitors.

He always encouraged me to have dessert by saying we'd split it. It took me three or four dinner dates to discover he wasn't a sweets person, but he wanted me to feel free to indulge. I ordered the "Governor's Cake," a chocolate slice of heaven baked by former governor Fife Symington. The idea of a Republican politician baking for me was appealing.

I had planned for us to go to the movies above the restaurant, but the timing was wrong, so we drove to Desert Ridge, near his place. He bought tickets for an action picture at a new theater. I suggested senior citizen tickets, as we were both at least fifty-five, but Casanova declined my suggestion, saying he didn't want to publicly acknowledge his age. He obviously had some issues.

We settled ourselves into our seats on the aisle of stadium seating after my obligatory stop at the rest room. It was a mixed crowd—families, friends, dates. We held hands, as did the couple next to us. I saw no other public displays of affection. Casanova was a tactile person, and I did enjoy his explorations of my hands and arms as the movie started. I rested my hand on his knee and played his penis like a piano with my fingertips.

The movie was violent, so I averted my eyes from the screen. Far from engrossed in the film, I decided to be much naughtier than my usual self and tickled my way up his thigh. Then I did some light exploring of his privates—over his clothes, of course. I was enjoying myself, knowing he was enjoying himself, too. Glancing up, I noticed the theater was not completely dark. In fact, it was only half dark. What kind of movie theater isn't completely dark for the feature presentation? I immediately withdrew my hands.

After the movie, I mentioned why I had so abruptly ended my tickling.

"I sure hope no one noticed," I whispered.

"Only the guy sitting next to you," Casanova said.

The blush started at my toes and traveled to the tips of my ears. "No, you're just kidding me," I finally said.

"No, he was definitely envious."

"Why didn't you say something?" I sputtered.

"What? Like I wanted you to stop?"

The moral of the story—If you're trying to break out of your conventional box, make sure you're ready for whatever ensues.

One time when he was home from Chicago, he told me he wouldn't be available. Although he said he didn't have to tell me, he explained that a teacher he dated in Chicago was going to be visiting. She knew about me, but not about F.

Flabbergasted that I wasn't angry, I was sure both F and the teacher were nice people. I wanted him for a limited relationship and didn't mind that he needed or wanted more than one relationship. In fact, so did I. I continued to date to find another guy like him. He was flattered when I mentioned it. I didn't want to put all my "emotional eggs" in one basket. After two marriages that ended in betrayal, I'd never give a man that much emotional power again.

A change came about when Casanova decided to be geographically monogamous. He dated only me in Phoenix and only the teacher in Chicago. I didn't make the same pledge to him.

We took many short trips—a romantic stay at a cabin in Greer in the White

Mountains of Arizona; a weekend seminar at the Lowell Observatory in Flagstaff when we stayed at the historic and haunted Monte Vista Hotel; an excursion to southeastern Arizona to see Kartchner Caverns, Tombstone and Singing Wind Bookstore, and adventures in New Orleans, and Washington D.C.

While on these trips, I noticed that he'd get into snits. Not with me, but with outside incidents such as dirty silverware at a restaurant or the lack of availability of a medicine he wanted at a Mexican *farmacia*. I let him fret his way through it and refused to take on his dark mood. He also didn't talk to his daughter who had married someone who wasn't Jewish, but he did send gifts to his granddaughter.

I thought all was well and was looking forward to the next trip I'd planned to Bisbee, Arizona. A week before we were to leave, he sent me a text. It read that he wouldn't be seeing me again because a girlfriend from California was moving in with him.

I felt blindsided. So, he had lied when he said he wasn't interested in a live-in relationship. Or had he changed over the two years we went out and I failed to notice the signs? I didn't love him, so I wasn't hurt badly. But I'd miss him and our good times. The only bad part was the way he ended it—by email instead of in person.. He didn't have the guts to face me.

   Would I find another man with whom to have a close but limited relationship?

   Lesson learned: Men may change their minds about what they want from a relationship without telling me.

Chapter Three
Scrabble Man

While I was dating Casanova, I continued to date other men. Scrabble Man was included in one of my twice-weekly batch of matches. Although I wasn't wild about his photo, I reminded myself how superficial looks were. We emailed back and forth until we found a time and place to meet—a Starbucks near Paradise Valley Mall. That was a trek for me, but dating takes effort.

Scrabble Man was already there when I arrived. He might have been my height. I couldn't tell because he was sitting down. With black curly hair and bright eyes, he looked exactly like his photo, but with a few more pounds. Who doesn't carry a few extra? Heavy bodies turn me on. Skinny bodies are a turnoff. Who wants to outweigh her date? I ordered an iced tea and we sat down to talk.

Scrabble Man was a New Yorker. He'd lived in Phoenix at least ten years, but the accent and attitude prevailed. Divorced, Scrabble Man had two daughters, one at ASU with such a terrific scholarship that he bought her a car, and the other still in high school. He gave me a clipping of a chess column he wrote for a New York Jewish newspaper.

"Do you play chess?" he asked with a smile.

"I play it well enough to know how the pieces move, but not with strategy."

His smile disappeared, and he dove into explaining his work. As the marketing director for a string of technical schools, he worked hard and long at his job, putting in night time hours, too. Personally, I'm over that. I'm retired so I can take short-term jobs that don't require overtime or stress.

"I worked for a technical school called Griswold Institute in Cleveland right after college," I said. "I worked in the high school side of the operation. *Finish high school in half the time* was its motto. Mostly I taught dropouts, Vietnam vets, people being vocationally rehabilitated, and rock star wannabes. It was quite an introduction to education. I'd thought I knew tough because I'd student-taught at an inner-city junior-senior high school in Rochester, New York, but Griswold had a heroin-shooting gallery on the back steps."

He changed the subject. "I've lived in this area the whole time I've been in Phoenix. My wife and I had a house close to here. When we separated, I rented an apartment nearby for six years. Recently I bought a condo, also in the area. I like it and I know it."

RIGID flashed through my mind. He didn't venture out of his neighborhood.

He asked me about my marriages. It's so difficult for me to do small talk. My sister advised me to mention one, not two marriages, and only one child—my youngest son who was still a teenager. *But what about my daughters who were killed in an airplane crash? What about my stepsons from my second marriage, whom I raised from the time they were six and nine? They were still a major part of my life.*

"I've been married twice," I said. "The first time for twelve years and the second time for fifteen years. I definitely do not want to get married again."

"Do you know the rules of dating?" he asked.

"Fill me in."

"I've been dating about four years," he said, scratching his chin. "Usually I meet for a drink or coffee first, like we did tonight. Then if both of us like what we hear and see, we go out the next week. Sex is saved for the third date."

I was speechless at this revelation. Did he see my jaw drop? Mandatory sex on the third date? I don't think so.

I switched the conversation to writing. He was thinking about writing some books on chess. We talked about book proposals, writing classes, and MFA programs. He said a colleague was interested in the latter. I promised to collect some information from a friend who was in a long-distance MFA program.

He asked if I played any games. I told him I played Scrabble with my mother every day and boasted that I had scored a five-hundred in a game. His ears visibly quivered and his eyes sparkled. That's when I noticed his thick neck. It was wider than his head. I never realized that I found wide necks unattractive.

"We'll have to play sometime," he said. "Have you played with any of the local clubs?"

"I've seen articles in the newspaper about them, but never ventured there," I replied.

"They are very serious," he said. "Have you ever used a timer?"

"No, Mom and I play a friendly game."

"When you use a timer, you have twenty-five minutes each to play the game. If you forget to turn off your timer, you can end up with no time and still have tiles to play."

"Hmm, interesting. As I said, I only play friendly games, not serious ones."

"As far as I'm concerned, a second date is in order," he announced.

Okay, only two weird warnings. His pronouncement of sex on the third date and possible rigidity. My eyes kept darting to his neck and not liking it, but that was so petty I had to rule that warning out.

"Sounds good to me," I said.

"How about dinner, then Scrabble at my place?" he asked.

"Okay." I reached for my calendar and checked for a free evening.

"How about next Tuesday? About seven?" I ventured.

"That works for me," he said. "I have focus groups every night this week."

He gave me his address and walked out with me, intending to accompany me to my car. Where was it? I was so embarrassed to forget where I parked my car. Maybe it was stolen. It's happened before after parking it for a few hours. I kept clicking the keyless entry and searching in the dark for the telltale rear lights. We circled the parking lot three times before I found it. He probably thought I was an airhead.

He opened the door to my car. Then he hugged me and gave me a quick kiss. Guess that's the rule for the first date.

From: Scrabble Man

To: Annie
Subject: Scrabble lists
*I've attached two lists: all the two-letter words
that can be made into three-letter words, and
all the three-letter words that can be made
into four-letter words, according to the third
edition of the Official Scrabble Dictionary. It's
only fair for you to have these, as I have
memorized 95% of them.*

From: Annie
To: Scrabble Man
Subject: Scrabble lists
*Are you into winning by intimidation? I'm a
social Scrabble player, not a tournament-type
of woman!*
Annie

From: Scrabble Man
To: Annie
Subject: Scrabble lists
*Don't be intimidated by these lists. They're the
most basic tiny words that players need to
know, whether they play socially or otherwise.
They are the building blocks of the game, and
every player should know them. But feel free
to have access to them by using these "cheat*

sheets" while playing. I figure just like there are tennis players and golfers who play socially, but nevertheless take lessons to improve their skill level and hence increase their enjoyment, same principle applies to the lists.

By the way, if you wanna see what top-level tournament play looks like, check out ESPN this Sunday at 1:30 to 2:30 pm. They'll be showing the Scrabble All-Stars tournament, featuring the top players in the country....

The next day a married friend and I were having a drink. I updated her on Scrabble Man.

"Maybe he's such a serious player he has a Scrabble board tattooed on his body," she suggested. "And you know where he positioned the 'triple word score.'"

"He's definitely not the tattoo type, but I would describe him as 'intense,'" I said.

"I'm worried about you going to play anything at his place. What do you really know about this guy?"

"His daughter who's in high school lives with him."

"How do you know she's going to be there?"

"It's a school night, for heaven's sakes."

"You're assuming she'll be there."

"What do you suggest?"

"Arrange to play the game at a coffeehouse or even a bar. You can't be too careful these days. It's not like you've been out with him a million times."

"He's intense about games. And this is only the second date. He said it's the usual thing to have sex on the third date."

"How do you know that's not just a ploy to lure you to his place?"

"Okay, okay, I'll think about it."

From: Annie
To: Scrabble Man
Subject: Scrabble date
I'm nervous about going to your place to play Scrabble. Friends have advised me to stick to a public place for a second date. How about dinner, then Scrabble at the Starbuck's where we met last time?

From: Scrabble Man
To: Annie
Subject: Scrabble date
I think you're worried about playing Scrabble with me. Why don't we just plan dinner and a movie if that will make you more comfortable .
. .

Date #2

I had already worn the outfit that made me look the thinnest to our first date. Should I go for casual comfy, professional, or sexy? I wasn't feeling any chemistry, so I went for casual comfy—black jeans, black tee shirt, and black and silver plaid shirt over the tee shirt.

I arrived on time and scanned the room, but he wasn't there. Two demerits for being late. I waved off the hostess and waited in the vestibule. After fifteen minutes, I was ready to leave, but checked my cell phone to make sure he hadn't left a message. Nothing. As I got up to go, Scrabble Man came in.

"Sorry I'm late. Things are hectic at work. They laid off one of my workers, and I must do both my job and his. But in this economy, I can't complain. At least I have a job."

The waitress seated us. I ordered a beer; he ordered water. He asked her about the fish. Fish? This was a pizzeria.

"I'm doing Atkins," he explained. "You would have been safe at my place. My daughter would have been there as a chaperone. Remember, we don't have sex until the third date."

Guess I wasn't going to get a pizza. I couldn't order a whole one for myself, even if I could eat it. I ordered eggplant parmesan with spaghetti.

I made the mistake of asking how his day was. I got a fifteen-minute dissertation on his woes at work. Two more demerits for negativity.

"So, this is our second date. We get to have sex on the next one," he gloated.

The next date was looking less likely every minute.

"I did a search on amazon.com," he said, "but didn't see any books listed except a picture book. Is that yours?"

"Yes, my first book was a picture book. You must have looked me up under Anne. All my other books are listed under Annie." Was he interested enough to check up on me?

"Oh, yeah, I'll try 'Annie' tomorrow."

Maybe I'll at least get some book sales out of this. I couldn't help it. Every time I tried to focus on his face, my eyes travelled to that fat neck. It made him look like a caricature. Was it the neck or a visceral reaction to the man?

The food was good, not great. He didn't take the check right away when the waitress brought it. Was I sharing the cost? His dinner was twice as much as mine. Should I be magnanimous and suggest we split the bill or tally up my share?

He glanced at me and then the check. I was about to say something when he took out his wallet and laid his credit card on the bill.

Should I reciprocate and throw down my credit card? After two awkward minutes, I decided to let him pay unless he said something to the contrary.

"What movie would you like to see?"

He was not like me. I would have planned a choice of a few movies and had the schedule with me.

"It's 8:30," I said. "Movies generally start at 7 and 9:30. I don't think I can stay up for the movie. Thank you for dinner."

"Oh, okay."

He walked me out to my car. This time I had memorized exactly where I'd left it. He grabbed me and thrust his tongue in my mouth. Blech! I wanted to gag, but I managed a polite smile and got into my car.

Definitely no third date. He didn't ask so I didn't have to turn him down.

Lesson learned: Don't have sex until after the third date. By that time, the guy may no longer be appealing.

Chapter Four
The Military Supplier

I decided to try a different dating site—Match.com, ready for a much larger site than jdate. The new site sent me emails every other day. Each email featured twelve guys whose profiles supposedly matched mine. I generally ignored them although I rarely deleted them. When I wanted some male interaction, I went back and opened those emails, sent a short message to two or three men who seemed like possibilities, telling them to look at my profile and email me if interested.

One night, a guy answered: *It is around 9:30 and I just checked my computer to see if you responded. This is my computer and I will check it again in the morning. I will wait around a few minutes tonight to see if you received this.*

I emailed him right back to let him know I hadn't received the original message. He replied with his phone number and asked me to call him. I printed out his profile to study it. His picture showed him in a tuxedo with a serious expression. Part of the profile said:

I am 63, athletic and toned, 6'1" tall . . . outgoing, intelligent, funny, perceptive, handsome, with spontaneous tendencies. Variety is the spice of life and it is boring to do the same thing every week. My sexuality is very much alive without medical help. The person I am looking for should be outgoing, attractive, and be a little like I have described myself. I smoke cigars occasionally but not in the presence of others, and I would prefer my date not smoke, but it is okay. I am interested in a long-term relationship and hopefully she is also. If not that's okay. I like people to be who they are and not try to change other's.(sic) As to relationships, they were so long ago they don't count anymore.

The man played golf, was a nine handicap, and lifted weights five times a week. He liked to attend plays, movies, concerts, and take weekend trips. The guy sounded okay for dating material, if a bit stuck on himself. Then I checked up on what he wanted in a date, the real test:

Someone tall (5'7" to 6') and body type average, athletic and toned, a few extra pounds, and curvy.

I fit the last two descriptions so I called him.

He suggested going out that evening. I was having a major allergy attack—sneezing, coughing, and losing my voice . How desperate was I? Pretty desperate for male companionship. Casanova had been out of town for almost six weeks.

My new chance for a romance, or at least sex in the future, overpowered my allergies. I agreed to meet at a local club at 8:30, so we'd have some time to get acquainted before the band started.

I dragged myself out of bed but didn't have the energy to take a shower or try on outfits—I just wore what was closest to the closet door. I did put some makeup on my puffy red eyes. Shuffling to my car, I drove the ten minutes to the club. My date was there, waiting.

Why do they all lie about their age? If this guy was sixty-three, he'd had a hard life. He looked closer to seventy-five. We talked, but I had to repeat everything several times. I was losing my voice and he needed a hearing aid. He talked about golf. I told him I knew how to play but wasn't an avid fan of the game. That didn't stop him from going on and on.

The guy said he owned the largest military surplus business in the state and lived in one of his rental homes near his store. He'd been engaged. When they broke up, they sold their home at Piestewa Peak. Was my head foggy, or did I remember from his profile that he hadn't had a relationship in a long time? Hm.

The Bad News Blues Band from Tucson rescued us from the frustration of carrying on a conversation since I couldn't speak and he couldn't hear. The band and their combination of blues and classic rock put me into a great mood. People were dancing—even the regular guy who danced on rollerblades and wore a baseball hat with a matching shirt that read *Fuck the police* was prancing around.

I was bopping my body up and down, but Mr. Military Supplier showed no interest in getting on the dance floor until a slow song came along. As he held me, I did feel chemistry. He was gentle and firm at the same time, which I thought was a good clue to bedroom behavior. We danced a few more songs, both fast and slow. At the end of the band's set, I was fading fast, so I told him I was going home. He walked me out to my car and kissed me gently with a passionate undertone.

I went home and crashed, not even bothering to take off my clothes.

When I woke up the next morning, I had no voice. I emailed him that I had had a good time the night before and could feel some chemistry, but I couldn't call him because I had no voice. He emailed back that he also enjoyed our date, hoped I'd get better soon, and to email him or call when I did.

On Monday, I went to the doctor first thing in the morning. My voice was still completely gone, and I had to give a seminar to twenty student teachers that afternoon. The doctor prescribed steroids. They did the trick. By four o'clock I could speak loudly enough to be effective for an hour and a half.

I was feeling better by Tuesday and called The Military Supplier. He wanted to see me that night. We agreed to meet at eight at a movie theater between our homes.

I went on the Internet to look up the show times, but they were listed as "unavailable." When I got to the theater, I found out why. Even though the place was next to the Ritz Carlton and across from the Biltmore shopping center, and it was high season for tourists, they showed no movies after seven on weekdays. I'd never encountered that before.

We decided to meet for a drink at Houston's, a nearby bar/restaurant. He talked more about golf. Mr. Military Supplier was in a singles golf group and a seniors golf group. I again told him that although I didn't hit out of bounds often, I played "pitch and piddle down the middle." I was the kind of golfer who threw the ball toward the hole when I became slow or frustrated. He didn't suggest we play golf.

I told him about myself, but he didn't appear to be listening. His eyes appeared to be fixed on my chest. After one drink, he walked me to my car and climbed in to see it. I had a Honda Civic Hybrid, so I'm used to people wanting to check out my car. No, I didn't plug it in at night. The gas engine recharged the electric engine.

He leaned over and kissed me. It felt good, but I felt overexposed in the brightly lit garage. He wanted to make out. Here was another guy with high school moves. I had to put on my assertive voice to say good night and end the date.

The Military Supplier did call and ask me to the movies for Friday night. It would be our third date. Remember Scrabble Man? I was horny as all get out, so sex was a possibility. I went to the drugstore and bought some condoms, knowing Military Supplier would think he was an extra-large.

We went to a "rush-hour" movie, the ones scheduled between four and six. He held my hand, caressed my arm, and kneaded my neck during the movie. My mojo was revved up by the time the credits rolled.

After the movie, he didn't suggest dinner. Was he cheap or was he too excited? He led me to his mucho, macho pickup truck—would he drive anything else?—and showed it off. I got in my car and followed him straight to his house. When I was barely in the front door, he guided me to the bedroom.

Foreplay was short but not sweet enough for me. Absolute silence prevailed. When I felt his "member," I understood the comment about sex in his profile. He was proud of his inordinately large and hard penis. It did feel good as it'd been a while since I'd been intimate with a man. Even though I went to the bathroom before we left the movie theater, I think his "member" deflated my bladder because the sheet was wet. I was mortified, but neither of us mentioned it.

I became more and more uncomfortable as he still didn't say a word. Then I became angry with myself. Why hadn't I stopped the action to give him a condom? He didn't mention using protection, either. That was the first time I'd had unprotected sex, and I had the feeling this guy was one that trolled the Internet dating sites to get sex. Shit! What had I exposed myself to?

I got up, gathered my clothes, and slipped into the bathroom. After I dressed, I went back to the bedroom and said good bye. He said he'd call. Did I want him to?

Over the course of the next few days, I decided I didn't want to see him again. He had a habit of calling at the last minute. There's spontaneous, and then there's thoughtless. He wasn't good enough in bed to justify a "body buddy" relationship. We had too little in common for a friendship.

He left a message a week later, wanting to get together that afternoon at his place and watch the PGA tournament on television. I'd been right. He hadn't listened to my disinterest in golf. More likely, he was just interested in a last-minute booty call. I left him a message that I was busy.

I never heard from him again, thank goodness.

But I needed to investigate my loss of urine during sex. I went to my OB-GYN who referred me to a specialist. He suggested physical therapy and it worked.

I was ready to try sex again.

Lesson learned: Don't let my passion overrule sensible precautions for sex.

Chapter Five
The Grease Man and the Night of Lasagna

I met The Grease Man through Match.com. His profile listed him as a six-foot-two inch, fifty-eight-year-old Phoenix man. His picture showed a nice smile. He wasn't thin—that's a good thing as I've mentioned. He said he was optimistic and was "looking for a special lady that is assertive in nature, outgoing, a great sense of humor, and has a great outlook on life." Okay, he's not an English major in that he used "that" instead of "who," but I'm not that picky. I knew a woman who eliminated guys as potential dates for bad grammar. The best part was that he didn't have a preference in body type. I never answer when the only body types preferences listed are "slim," "athletic," or "a few extra pounds." I've got way more than a few extra pounds.

We corresponded via the Internet for about a week before we met. He refused to make definite plans because he was a salesman and all over town during the day.

We set a day, Thursday, and a time, noon, to arrange to meet. A little weird.

I was getting a manicure when he called and wanted to meet an hour earlier than we had planned. Racing home, I slapped on makeup and threw on an outfit. I still made it to the Taco Bell on time but didn't see anyone who fit his description. It was 11, too early for lunch for me, and I'm not a Taco Bell person, preferring family-owned Mexican restaurants. I bought a diet soda and sat down to wait.

I waited long enough to admit I'd been stood up when he sauntered in, resembling his amiable photo from the website. He sat down and apologized for being late. His sales call took longer than planned. We talked, but I didn't get a good sense of who he was. I learned he lived in a nice section of town. He sold grease and oil to school districts, hospitals, and the like.

He mentioned "cuddling" several times. Did he intend the phrase as a euphemism for sex, or was he the teddy bear he projected? We didn't eat lunch, just talked. I got good vibes from him. Before we parted, we made a date to walk around the Biltmore golf course on Saturday morning.

On Friday night, about ten, I was on my drive home from the movie/sex date with The Military Supplier, when I got a call from The Grease Man on my cell phone. He canceled our walking date because the forecast called for rain. He didn't suggest breakfast somewhere, but he did invite me to help him prune his hedges. I informed him that I paid someone to do that for me and wasn't interested in landscape maintenance, especially if it was going to rain. We made no specific plans to see each other again.

A week later, I got a message from The Grease Man. I returned his call but got his voicemail, so I left a message. He didn't call back.

Was this guy shy, married, or not interested?

A few weeks later I was entertaining my college-aged niece when he called. He said to get in touch with him after she left. I did call him a few days later.

"We probably should go on a hike," he said. "I need to get more active so I look better."

"You look fine to me," I said.

"I do? Then how about I cook lasagna for you? You bring the movie."

It was against my better judgment as I should have learned something from the incident, "When Passion Overcomes Common Sense." I was horny and he seemed so huggable. When he gave me the directions to his place, I learned he lived in a guest house.

Why did a man in his late fifties live in a guest house?

I went to the library and agonized over what movie to bring. Most of the recent releases I'd either seen or had made a conscious decision not to see them. I went through the comedy section and found one called *Once Upon a Time in the Midlands*, made by the same people who did *The Full Monty*, which I enjoyed. I also grabbed two of my favorite comedies from my own collection, *Ace Ventura, Pet Detective* and *The Mask*. I did the usual "miracle job," meaning a shower, hair touch-up, makeup, and at least eight costume changes before I settled on the right outfit, alluring but not flashy or trashy.

His place was easy to find, and I arrived at six, the appointed time. He met me at the door in gym shorts and an old tee shirt. Weird. I guess he didn't think he needed to clean up for me. He gave me the grand tour of his bedroom, living room, kitchen, and bathroom. It was rather cluttered with boxes and equipment piled everywhere. I met his two cats who were cute.

The Grease Man offered me some wine, but could only find one wine glass. A mound of clean dishes sat near the sink, ready to fall if one was moved. He told me that he had been up until midnight last night doing dishes. Uh-oh. Slob or depressed?

The wine was quite good, and I needed something to relax me, so I drank it faster than I should have. We sat at the kitchen table and talked. He asked me to define words I used in normal conversation, a lot of them, like "lout," "repudiate," and "abysmal."

I did get more information about him, but it could be interpreted several ways. He'd been married once for two years and had been seeing a woman for three years, but they broke up about a year ago. His mother, now eighty-one, was widowed four years ago and wanted to sell her house, but he didn't want her to, as it was valuable. She wanted him to move in so he could maintain the place for her. He didn't want to move in with his mother, so she built the guest house for him.

Possibilities:

1. He's a caring guy who wants his independence.
2. He's a greedy guy interested only in his mother's money.
3. He has a problem with commitment except to his mother.

I deliberated on the verdict.

He got up to check the lasagna—a frozen entrée. I thought he was showing some interest in me by taking the time and effort to cook. His stock was going down, especially after he made the cats a custom dinner and heated it in the microwave oven.

The next time he checked the lasagna, the top layer of cheese and noodle slid off. It landed partly on the rack, partly on the bottom of the oven. He was flummoxed, so I made light of it. I suggested that he finish heating our dinner in the microwave. He acted like I was a genius. His stock went down further.

We returned to wine and conversation. Grease Man was taken aback that I was a feminist. He had missed the entire women's movement as far as I could tell from his idea of what a feminist was.

Finally, the remains of the lasagna were ready. He proceeded to set the table with Styrofoam-sectioned plates, napkins and plastic forks. Why plastic when real dishes were piled up next to the sink? He glanced at the Styrofoam, then at me, and commented that he didn't want to have to wash any more dishes. So much for making an extra effort for me. I should note that there was no salad, vegetable, bread, or accompaniment of any type with the lasagna. Obviously, dinner and the clean-up didn't take long.

The only place to view the movie was in his bedroom. He chose *Once Upon a Time in the Midlands* from the DVDs I'd brought. The bed held many pillows, so I propped myself up expectantly. The Grease Man fast-forwarded through all the previews. The actors' English or Scottish thick accents were hard to understand, not that I had much of a chance to try.

He lay down on the bed. Rather than cuddling, he plopped his hand on my rather large boob. I told him he was going a bit fast for me. Grease Man retreated to hugging for a while, then he kissed me on my neck. This got me in the mood. He attempted to unhook my bra, but after much fumbling still couldn't unfasten it. I laughed, then reached back and undid it. Why? I was horny, that's why. The foreplay lasted five minutes. I excused myself to go to the bathroom, stopping by my purse on the way back.

"I can't feel anything if I use one," he said.

"You definitely won't feel anything if you don't," I answered.

"I don't even know how to put one on," he said.

"Oh, you don't have to worry about that, I'll put it on for you," which I did to his dismay.

It was over quickly.

"Well, this certainly makes it less messy," he said as he examined at the used condom on his penis.

It's a good thing I saw the evidence, or I wouldn't have known that he came. The sex was not satisfying.

He went into the bathroom. I got cold waiting for him to reappear and reached over for one of his tee shirts stacked beside the bed. I worried that he was so bummed out by wearing a condom that he'd drowned himself in the toilet. But Grease Man finally returned to the bedroom, stooped to the floor, picked up my clothes, and set them on the bed.

I joked, "Is that a subtle hint to leave?" He didn't laugh.

After an awkward silence, he said he had to check on the cats. I got the message, so I threw on my clothes and ejected the movie from his player. Grease Man was in the kitchen, cleaning the stove. He turned to me and said, "The whole evening went bad when the cheese slid off the lasagna. It's going to be so hard to clean it up. But I guess I'll be the one do it."

Damned right you are.

"I'll walk you out to your car," he said.

Whoop-de-do.

"I almost forgot," he said. "I have a present for you in my car."

He opened the trunk and handed me a Styrofoam egg container with life-sized chocolate marshmallow eggs. "They're really good," he said. "I bought some for myself, too."

I thanked him, got in my car, and drove away. It was only eight-thirty, and I was dressed to go out but didn't want to go by myself. I called my neighbor, the Barbie Doll look-alike, but she didn't answer her cell phone. I stopped at Baskin Robins and ordered a scoop of Chocolate Mousse Royale.

When I arrived home, my neighbor called to say she would be home shortly and would love to meet me for a drink. Her date was also already over. Since it was still early, I knew there was a good story behind that one.

We went to a Scottsdale hangout, The Sugar Shack. I told her about my evening, and then she shared about her evening. She'd been going out with this man for about five months. He was well-heeled, and traveled in the same circles as she did before her divorce. She always had fun times with him at charity events at the Arizona Country Club and other places, but she had misgivings. He was short on good looks, and he couldn't get it up anymore. But those were things she could live with. He had the trappings of a guy she wanted to date.

"At our age, everybody's got something wrong with them," she said. "You have to figure out if you're willing to put up with whatever it is. Ugly and bad sex I can deal with. But he drinks too much. I've had to take him home and put him to bed more than once. Tonight, I went to meet him about seven, but he was already so far gone that our friends suggested I take him home. I'm not going to put up with that. Here we are at nine o'clock on a Friday night and our dates are over."

We shared some nachos.

As I ruminated over the night, what came to mind was Aretha Franklin singing, "Respect."

Lesson learned: I'd let my horniness overpower my judgment. I hadn't shown myself respect. That wasn't going to happen again.

Chapter Six
Baby Boomers Schmoes Still Looking for Barbie

I had tried speed dating once and it was a total disaster. Most of the people were half my age, and all the guys rejected me. I made myself sign up for another speed-dating event before a singles dance because the attendees would be more in my age range. The speed dating would serve as an introduction, so I'd have someone to talk to during the dance. The event cost twenty dollars, but that included the seven-dollar dance afterward.

I knew I wasn't into it when I waited until the last minute to get ready. No agonizing over my choice of clothing this time—I just put on what I'd worn to other dates.

I arrived a few minutes late, unusual for me when I'm hyped or excited about an event. Many of the other participants arrived even later, so I had fifteen minutes to get nervous.

The event was in the large back room, probably used for meetings, of a trendy restaurant. It had no decorations and seemed sterile.

Women sat at each of the six tables and the men rotated after five minutes of conversation.

The first man assigned to my table was skeleton-thin but engaging. He had traveled extensively in Europe and had four children, aged fourteen to twenty. Chemistry was lacking. However, I've enough experience to know that chemistry was overrated as an initial criterion for dates. With less than a minute, I jotted down notes, so I'd talk knowledgably with the man if I saw him at the dance.

Date #2 had thick, grey hair. I talked more than he did so I discovered only that he worked at the VA hospital and had lived in Phoenix one year.

Date #3 was familiar, though he showed no recognition of me. We talked enough for me to realize we had worked at the same school district at the same time. I remembered that he was quite handsome when he was younger, but gravity changed his face quite a bit. Our five-minute talk was friendly.

Date #4 looked younger than I, was handsome, and obviously not interested in me. He talked the whole time about being a youth soccer coach.

The next man up worked for the National Park Service at a monument near Phoenix. He was tall, bald, and I got good vibes from him. We had a mutual acquaintance. He wanted to talk about what would be the right school districts to approach for the outdoor education he had dreamed up. I liked him and would seek him out later.

The last man was proud of working sixty hours a week for thirty-five years. He had a great desire to be a grandpa, but none of his children had provided him the opportunity. He seemed type A and uninterested in me.

The speed dating time was up and we headed to the bar where the dance was going to start. I wanted to cultivate some men as friends, but I'd not found any willing. They wanted to date or forget it.

A nearly bald guy with a red shirt, stuck up a conversation with me as I got a drink at the bar. He was tall and solid, my type of attractive. He seemed nice and asked me for my phone number. I gave it to him but then he melted into the crowd.

I sat at a table next to the park ranger, but he made it abundantly clear that he was not interested. He was tall and skinny. Was he repulsed by a plus-size woman?

I moved to the bar and Date #3 sat next to me. We had a nice conversation. He bragged about how much more money he made since quitting teaching and going into the business world. The guy then said he liked to date teachers because they carried on intelligent conversations. This seemed promising. His son lived in my neighborhood, and he insisted that my son was the one whom his son talked about all the time. Could be, I supposed. He also told me how beautiful his wife was, but how he tired of her when he realized how shallow she was. Hmm, was this man saying that the package was more important than the wrapping?

My neighbor arrived on schedule. In her late thirties, tall, blond, and gorgeous, she was a nice person and a great mother. She was the image of a Barbie doll. She wasn't not aware of her good looks and was shy and humble.

I glanced over to see Date #3 salivating. When a guy asked her to dance, Don gave me his card and asked me to put in a good word for him.

I wanted to say, "hell, no!" but I didn't. How rude. Here this guy was talking to me for thirty minutes at a singles dance, and seemed to be enjoying himself. At the first sight of Barbie, I was chopped liver to her prime filet. Now I could understand if Date #3 was a Ken-type himself, but he wasn't. He was twenty years older than my neighbor and not great-looking or suave.

The other men also fell over themselves for my neighbor, none of whom were gorgeous or her age. What was the deal? Hadn't baby boomer men learned that the exterior—their own and others—was transitory, and the inside was so much more—or less?

The night was depressing. It seems I have a choice—lose eighty pounds to look more like Barbie or stay out of the dating game and eat chocolate.

Dove Bars, anyone?

Lesson learned: Speed dating was just a chance to get rejected many times in one night.

Chapter Seven
Mr. Phone Sex

My middle son, who was twenty-three at the time, informed me about the "men's rules of calling." If a man calls within the first twenty-four hours of meeting a woman, it shows he's desperate. If he calls in forty-eight hours, he really likes the woman. If he's not sure he wants to date the woman, he waits three days. R----, the almost bald guy with a red shirt I met at a singles dance, called thirty-six hours later.

We made a date for dinner on Friday night at a restaurant near my home.. I was a cautious dater, meaning I didn't want him to know where I lived. On Friday night we became better acquainted over sea bass. A few things he said gave me pause:

1. He was married twice. He never lived with his second wife because he was transferred to Germany, and she decided not to follow him.

2. He moved to Arizona to take care of his mother. I thought that might be something

we had in common, since I visited my mom every day in her assisted-living home.

"I make her dinner every night. If I don't, she won't eat," he said.

"Is she bedridden?" I asked.

"No, she just expects me to do it."

Ding, ding, ding, the warning bells were sounding in my head.

    *   *   *   *

    *

After dinner we went to La Posada, a resort in Paradise Valley that featured a live band. We danced both the fast and the slow dances. He did his "dirty dancing" act and I ate it up. I felt sexy and desirable without guilt.

We strolled out to the parking lot. He asked me to join him in his car for a kiss. I was game. His kiss brought the thrill. We necked passionately. When he tried to grope me, I resisted.

"You're coming on way too strong," I said.

"Okay, I'll back off. It's your job to be the one to say 'no,'" he said.

How high school.

I jumped in my car and headed home, shaking my head all the way.

    *   *   *

It was eleven. on a hot Saturday night. I passed by my phone and saw the message light blinking. Could it be R----? He'd called at ten-twenty and asked that I phone him back. I was hesitant to phone anyone after ten at night, but I called him anyway.

"Where are you in the house?" he asked.

"I'm in the living room, why?"

"Please go into your bedroom."

This was a strange request, but I didn't see any reason not to.

"Lock the door," he ordered.

This was starting to sound even stranger, but it was only a phone call, for heaven's sakes.

"The door is locked. Do you have a deep dark secret to tell me?" I teased.

"What are you wearing?" he asked.

I wasn't about to tell him I had on a faded, cotton housedress, covered with flowers.

"Shorts and a tee shirt," I lied. I never wear shorts. Not only do the veins in my legs proclaim their existence for all to see at a hundred yards, but my thunder thighs are not for public viewing.

"Take your clothes off and get naked on your bed," he said.

Setting the phone down, I quickly followed orders, but cheated and donned the oversized tee shirt I wear to bed.

"Are you naked?" he asked.

"Yes," I lied.

"I am, too. You are so hot I can't wait to see you. How about some phone sex?"

"I've never done this before," I admitted. I was sure I wasn't going to, either.

"Describe to me where you are."

"I'm lying on my four-poster bed, on top of the red silk comforter I bought in China."

"I'm on my bed and I don't have any clothes on. My cock is hard for you."

Shock and discomfort filled me. So why didn't I hang up?

"Come on, baby," he whispered. "You know you want it."

I decided to play it to the max.

"Oh yeah," I moaned.

"Are you touching yourself in just the right place?"

"It feels great," I lied. I was way too horny if I was turned on by this weirdo's words. But part of me wanted to follow his instructions, just to see what phone sex was like.

"Let me put it inside," he said.

Inside where? We're on the telephone, I wanted to shout. But I didn't.

"How're you doing, baby?" he asked.

I decided to try to freak him out. "I already came."

"Wow. I haven't yet, but it's big and hard. What do you think it looks like?"

"A red mushroom on steroids."

"Oh, you're good, baby. It's sticking straight up for you."

I heard some moans and yips.

"It's coming, baby. It's coming."

Weird.

"So how did you like that?" he asked.

"I'm not comfortable with the whole phone sex idea." A little late to be saying this, of course.

"It's just the male role," he explained. "I've wanted to fuck you since the moment I saw you. You know you're sexy."

"I'm feeling really uncomfortable."

"I know you'll enjoy it more as we get to know each other better. I want you. I need you."

"You're scaring me."

"What's the matter, baby? I thought you were having fun."

"You may be too weird for me," I said.

"Oh, it was just for fun. When are we going dancing again? How about Friday night?"

Was he too weird or was he okay to meet somewhere? I did love to dance and listen to live music. If I met him there, I could always leave whenever I wanted. So, I agreed to the date. He told me to meet him at a night club in north Scottsdale. I'd never been there before.

*   *   *
*

The parking lot was jammed, and I had to park far away from the front door, where Mr. Phone Sex was waiting for me. We were early enough that most people were dining, and there was no cover charge. The band hadn't started yet, so we strolled around the huge restaurant and bar, both inside and out. It was the scene to see and be seen.

The band started playing, and immediately the dance floor was covered with people. Major jewels adorned both men and women, and those little linen outfits many of the women wore cost three-hundred dollars for each piece. Despite this, the people sported smiles on their faces and honestly seemed to enjoy the terrific music and the electric atmosphere. We danced for forty minutes nonstop, as did everyone else.

When the band took a break, Mr. Phone Sex managed to get us two soda waters. We collapsed into chairs at the now-empty dining tables.

"Have you told your friends that you have a boyfriend?" he asked.

I was taken aback. This was our second date. And I was seeing Cassanova.

"I have told some friends about you," I said. "but I didn't describe you as my boyfriend. We've just started going out."

"You mean you might go out with other men while you go out with me?"

"Possibly," I said, without admitting I already was.

"You wouldn't sleep with anyone but me."

This came across as a demand, not a question. "I might," I said. "I'm careful, however, and always use protection, in case you're worried about diseases."

"I just can't believe you would do that. You seemed like a nice, moral woman."

Was this the same guy who initiated phone sex last weekend?

"I am a nice, moral woman. I'm not interested in getting married. And I'm also not interested in putting all my emotional eggs in one basket." Wow. Where did that come from? It could be true. And do men have to justify dating more than one woman?

He said nothing for a while. We finished our sodas.

"I'm ready to go," he said. "I'll walk you to your car."

I was glad he accompanied me to the outer reaches of Mongolia, where my car stood without the benefit of a parking lot light. He didn't kiss me.

"Good night," he said.

I never heard from him again. Thank goodness. Now I know I didn't care for phone sex or possessive men.

Lesson learned: Avoid phone sex and possessive men.

Chapter Eight
The Fix-Up

In all the years I've been single, I had only one fix-up. The Fix-Up (TFU) happened when I was about two years into dating. A friend of mine was at a carwash and talked to a guy who mentioned he wanted to date but was not interested in marriage. She immediately thought of me and gave the guy my cell phone number, although she called to warn me he might call.

And call he did, within the hour. We spoke briefly and agreed to meet the next Friday night at Eli's, a nightclub in Scottsdale. We arranged to meet at eight, in order to have a few minutes to converse before the band started to play. I wrote his name in my calendar to ensure I would remember it. He'd be wearing a jacket that looked like an American flag. I'd wear something purple, my favorite color.

On the evening of the date, I made a fresh pot of loose-leaf tea leaves and had a few—okay, seven—chocolate chip cookies while I pondered what to wear. After my snack, I tried on many clothes. Nothing purple looked hot, so I decided on black pants, a tank top, and a purple-patterned silk shirt. When I checked the mirror, I could see my panty line. I tried it without panties, but felt naked.

I did a load of wash so I could wear panties that fit perfectly and showed no line. While I waited for the wash to be done, I read a John Sanford mystery and chowed down on roast chicken and more chocolate chip cookies. Then I transferred necessities from my everyday purse to my dance purse, one I could wear so I didn't leave valuables at my seat when I went out on the dance floor. Did men go through these pre-date preparations?

When I arrived at Eli's, all the tables were occupied. I hovered by the front door, my hands fidgeting. I went in and circled the bar, and two guys introduced themselves. Maybe I would stay if The Fix Up (TFU) didn't show. I bought myself a Long Island Iced Tea to calm my nerves, and stood by the front door, feeling anxious.

TFU arrived on time, wearing a sweater-jacket with the flag woven in the back. He was about my height. TFU was stocky, the body type I prefer. His full head of black and white hair was cut short and straight, and he wore black glasses. He had a trimmed mustache, mostly black. Handsome in that Robert Redford/Glen Campbell kind of way, he reminded me of my first husband.

TFU ordered a straight shot of something golden, and then we sat on the band platform. I asked him about his work, sheet metal forming. He said they had a big job and he'd have to work the next day. Hmm, clever way to have an early-out for a date. My job never came up.

I asked him if he had been married and got quite a saga. He had married at sixteen. When he came back from Vietnam, his wife didn't like him. They'd married so young that change was inevitable. TFU married a second time to a psycho. He had a daughter whom he hadn't seen since she was five because the ex-wife made visitation impossible. He married a third time on the rebound to a rich woman. I found out through more conversation that the first marriage was six years, the second one lasted six months, and the third one weathered one month. One of his wives had a brother or uncle who was in the slammer for money laundering and was part of a Columbian drug cartel.

The band moved on stage, so we found some bar stools in the pool-table area. The band was loud, making it difficult to talk. He pulled out his cigarettes and a box of cinnamon Altoids. We munched on the latter, but he didn't light up a cigarette. This was before the Arizona smoking ban.

The first song was a swing kind of thing. I was getting a bit worried about the band. I'd been to Eli's once before with a friend, and the band always played classic rock or rhythm and blues.

Finally, the band settled into some Motown tunes, and I suggested we dance. He was uncomfortable on the floor for someone who wanted to go dancing. There were quite a few people whirling around, so it wasn't like we were on display. I excused myself to go to the restroom after the dance.

Because of the noise, TFU had to shout to me in the pool-table area. I heard all about his family. He bought me a Diet Coke and water for himself, explaining that he didn't drink much because his father was an alcoholic. He didn't want to drink and drive because he'd killed enough people in Vietnam. Hmm, I thought he said he was a medic there. Ding, ding, ding went the warning bell.

He shared that his younger brother, a police officer in San Diego, had been killed, but didn't elaborate on whether it was job related. TFU talked quite a bit about Vietnam, his health problems since the war, and his

71

Purple Heart. I did little talking, an anomaly for me.

He complained about the music, explaining that he only liked hard rock. We danced once more. I suggested that we adjourn to a nearby fast food restaurant to talk since we were drinking nonalcoholic beverages and straining our voices to be understood.

The cold outside air infiltrated my thin clothes. I'd been prepared to dance until I sweated for hours. We headed toward the main street and went west a block. He talked more about his various careers and marriages. Strains of music from another band met our ears.

We discovered a nearly empty place called The Sozzle Grill. The band was outside. Three people sat at the table in front of us, employees of the restaurant who were off duty. One was the chef, a portly guy with a kind face. Another was a blond woman in her late twenties, too young to know the music being played. A guy at the table was drinking enormous martinis. Three other people lounged in gigantic beanbag chairs, definitely tourists.

The band asked what we wanted to hear. TFU suggested, "Smoke on the River." The band did a great rendition. Someone else suggested a Dylan song, "Knock, Knock,

Knocking on Heaven's Door." I was enjoying myself. The restaurant employees were rocking, too—downing many drinks and dancing to the music.

Then TFU asked the blonde to dance. The girl knew how shabby this was and insisted that I dance with the chef. I was fuming. How fast could I dump this guy? I was willing to overlook the smoking and the fixation on Vietnam, but I drew the line at him asking someone else to dance.

I told the guy it was time for me to go home. As we headed back to my car, he smoked a cigarette. I dodged his effort to kiss me. He said he'd call but didn't. And I was happy not to have to confront him about his bad behavior. TFU was history.

No one has fixed me up since then. Maybe it's for the best.

Lesson Learned: Avoid well-meaning advice from acquaintances about a friend they'd like you to meet.

Chapter Nine
One Date Wonders

Why did so many encounters last for only one date? I wasn't upset, but curious. My criteria for a second date was that the man showed some inkling that we could be friends. That, to me, was the bottom line. Even chemistry wasn't a requirement.
Incompatibility was the main reason I didn't settle for a second date, but I had no idea why the guy didn't want one.

I met Mr. Late through match.com. His profile didn't shout "crazy." He was smiling in his picture. We emailed a few times and agreed to meet for lunch. I told him where my part-time job was that day and asked him to pick a place for lunch. He emailed back that he scouted it out and picked Pizza Hut.

I went to the Pizza Hut he suggested, but it was just for take-out. After waiting fifteen minutes past the appointed time, I left my cell phone number with the counter person and went to a nearby McDonald's. Mr. Late called about twenty minutes later and met me there.

We had a good conversation for an hour on a great number of issues, and I was beginning to think this might merit a second date. Then he mentioned that one of his passions was studying the Bible as a guide to life. He went to Bible conferences and took his spiritual life seriously. He was a perfectly nice guy, but not for me, as I was not a religious person.

I met Mr. Intellectual through jdate. He was shorter than I, and chunky, but I decided to be a grown-up about a man's height. We chatted on the phone for more than an hour before we made a date to meet. During our conversation, I sensed he was a bit of a braggart. One, he belonged to MENSA. Two, he made a lot of money. Three, he had a great stylist, and four, he liked to go shopping and buy women jewelry and clothes, but I figured his bragging could be put down to nerves. He was also a conservative Republican, but not nasty when we disagreed.

I met him for lunch at The Cheesecake Factory. The other diners' conversations were loud, but I was able to tune them out. We had a great hour-and-a-half conversation. He wasn't a bit braggy. Mr. Intellectual wanted to date an intelligent woman, but I think he really meant someone smart but not as smart as I. When I kept up with him on topics and vocabulary, he was surprised. He never called back, and it disappointed me. I could blame it on my weight, but he was at least as overweight as I was. Perhaps my intelligence threatened him? Something else?

I arranged to meet Mr. Organ Recital for a drink at a Mexican restaurant. His profile said he was sixty-two, six feet tall and had liberal political tendencies. This last fact attracted me in this conservative state. He was into archeology, paleontology, dancing, dining, and fine wine. His photography had won several awards. He had traveled extensively, but still wanted to explore Australia, and the Aztec and Inca ruins.

Mr. Organ Recital was a little late, so I paid for my soda before he arrived. He wasn't particularly attractive, but that's not a make-or-breaker for me. He was thin, but I overlooked that. The first warning bell came when he made little eye contact during our conversation. He said that he had been placed in a TB sanatorium at a young age, then foster homes until he was adopted at eleven years old. He indicated that his biological parents were still alive.

The second warning bell went off when he described in detail what he ate every day. When he got to listing his illnesses, I knew we were not a match. I thanked him and rushed out the door.

Mr. Monologue's profile said he was sixty-three, with a few extra pounds, and recently moved to Carefree, which is a small town north of Phoenix. He was not sold on marriage, loved to cuddle, and was looking for a well-educated, gentle heart. Wasn't that a good description of me? We decided to meet for lunch at a restaurant at Desert Ridge, about midway between us. He emailed me if I was late, I would lose out on kisses. Hmm. I usually met guys just for a beverage, but I accepted the lunch date.

Mr. Monologue was already there when I arrived. He was friendly and had a nice smile. Conversation was easy. The man had recently moved to Arizona from Hawaii, after retiring from the military because his brother lived here. He had purchased a motor home with the intention of traveling with his wife, but she died shortly after the purchase. I was nonplused to find out he didn't live in Carefree, but in Sun Lakes, a senior community in the east valley, the opposite direction of Cave Creek. I never received a satisfactory answer about how this mistake found its way into his profile.

Then the monologue started. I learned everything about his life: work, marriage, children, brother, parents—the whole wordy ball of wax. He didn't ask any questions of me, nor gave me an opening to offer any information about myself.

After an hour, he did ask if I liked fishing. I said yes. He proposed a fishing trip. I assumed he meant to one of the local lakes, but I wasn't sure I wanted to spend that much time with him. However, I had been chiding myself for being too picky and not giving men a chance. I agreed to the date.

He walked me out to my car and asked if I wanted to go to the Grand Canyon fishing that weekend.

"The Grand Canyon? That's at least four-and-a-half hours away."

With an easy smile, he said, "Good, we'll make it a weekend trip."

"You're moving way too fast for me." I jumped in my car and raced away. He was obviously looking for a booty call, and I wasn't in the mood. I wasn't up for a long weekend, at least not with Mr. Monologue. I could imagine him talking the whole way to The Grand Canyon, and unlike *The Tonight Show*, I couldn't turn him off. And Casanova was in town.

Mr. Lean Times from Glendale was interested in dating women fifty-three to seventy-three. He liked any body type. I liked the way he thought. He identified himself as having a few extra pounds. Okay by me. He didn't drink at all, which always elicited the specter of a former alcoholic or a fundamentalist in religion. We emailed a few times and decided to meet for coffee. I suggested a bakery near the university where I worked part-time.

When I arrived, Mr. Lean Times was already there, nursing a cup of coffee. He asked me what I wanted to drink, and I told him any kind of black tea. He didn't listen well, and I ended up with an herbal tea, which I despise. I tried it anyway but as soon as the liquid hit my tongue, it recoiled.

I should have read the profile more carefully. When I returned home, I noticed that his favorite books were self-help books, and his favorite author was Art Linkletter.

We got right down to who we were and what we did. He was an accountant from Tucson, who'd been laid off about five years ago and hadn't worked a permanent job since. He worked temporary jobs through an agency. Mr. Lean Times had moved to Phoenix in hopes of permanent employment, but it hadn't happened yet. He had finally gotten his own place, a trailer.

I was a little leery of his precarious economic circumstances but called myself to task. Since I didn't want to have a monogamous relationship, it didn't matter how much he had unless he couldn't afford splitting our dating expenses. I thought we hit it off.

I don't know what he didn't like about me, but he didn't call or email again. My weight? My intelligence? My financial independence? My personality? That's what makes the one-date wonders tough. What was it about me that they didn't like?

Mr. No Chemistry was an insurance salesman. Liberal in his politics, he had a teenager at home at a time when I did, too. I met him at a Starbucks. We had a nice conversation. His daughter was a rascal, like my son. We traded war stories of parents of teenagers. We talked politics. In fact, we talked for almost two hours, but there was no chemistry. I mentioned that if we didn't date, I'd still be interested in becoming friends. He either didn't like me or was offended at my suggestion. I was disappointed I never heard from him again.

I met Mr. Liar through match.com and we emailed a few times. His profile said he was sixty, in real estate, and well-traveled. He wanted to meet, and he gave me his number on Thursday morning. I called him Friday and left a message. He called me Friday afternoon and asked where I was.

"I'm at the store with my son," I said.

"My daughter, who's sixteen, is returning from California tomorrow with her mom. I get to see her then," he said.

"How coincidental," I said. "My son is going to a movie with his dad tonight."

"Do you have plans tonight, or can we meet for a drink?" he asked.

"Good timing," I said. "Where and when?"

"How about seven tonight at AZ88? It's on---"

"I know where it is," I interrupted. AZ88 is a trendy place decorated ultra-modern by the Scottsdale Civic Center Mall.

"It's one of my favorite places," he said. "I'll be dressed casual."

That meant he would be wearing shorts. "I'll see you at seven," I said.

I had enough time to wash my hair and ponder my attire. Casual, okay. Shorts in public in a date situation? Never. I found black pants we used to call pedal pushers and paired it with a black tank top and a gauze shirt. It looked casual enough.

I arrived a few minutes early, but he was there. We immediately recognized each other from our web-based pictures.

"They're jammed inside," he said. "How about sitting outside?"

"That's fine," I said, not really meaning it. The sun was still strong, and it was over a hundred degrees. At least we found a table in the shade of three large metal pieces that looked like banana leaves. Otherwise, I would have melted in all that black.

We ordered drinks and started to chat; at least he did. He bragged about his job, dropped names, and thought he was ever so smooth. I wasn't impressed. He was not sixty, needed to have his hair re-colored, and his neck said he had to be at least seventy-five.

Mr. Liar asked where I lived, so I told him in the Arcadia area without giving out my address. He told me where he lived, and I knew he was a fake. The area was downscaled for Scottsdale. I was tired of his bull and ready to leave, fully understanding that I wasn't flashy or thin enough to be his type, thank God.

Then Mr. Liar said something that told me he was a married man.

"I have to pick up my daughter at her play rehearsal. She's involved in a summer theatre program." He'd told me earlier that his daughter was in California and wouldn't be back until tomorrow. I assumed he was sandwiching me in between work and his home life.

Mr. Liar offered to walk me to my car, but I declined. Good riddance.

Chapter Ten
Cruising Solo or Annie Get Your Rum

My responsibilities at home were becoming overwhelming. My teenaged son was driving me nuts, and I had to move my mom into an assisted living facility where I visited her daily. Needing some time alone, I investigated "Single Cruises."

I found a site called "Vacations to Go (VTG). Its idea of a singles cruise was to have people self-identify as singles, join for a fee, and then the group was added to a regular cruise.

I couldn't convince any friends to accompany me. The cruise was sailing in less than a month. How much did I want to go? Enough to go by myself? If so, I had to decide whether to be matched with a roommate or pay extra for a single cabin. They might pair me with a crazy for what would become the "Vacation from Hell." I spent the extra bucks and booked a single room.

There was a closed chat room through Yahoo to get to know the other one-hundred-ten single cruisers. I filled out a short profile, posted my picture, and received a daily digest of messages. It was reassuring to see that normal people had signed up for the cruise.

I liked the daily itinerary—breakfast at nine, an eleven o'clock mingle activity, a cocktail party almost every night before dinner, and dinner together. Most of the cocktail parties were themed: mad hatter, fifties, karaoke, Hawaiian, plus a cabin crawl, where people hosted cocktail parties in their cabins.

I realized I would have to wear a bathing suit. (I should mention that I'd gained fifty pounds in the last two years.) After trying on a few, I remembered my major problem with bathing suits, besides looking fat. I have enormous boobs. They fit in the suits, but gravity drags the suit down. Hence the big question—Would my boobs free themselves from the suit when I jumped into the waves from a snorkeling boat, re-boarded, or while dolphins pulled me in the water? X-rated images of me and the dolphins due to a swimsuit malfunction floated in my thoughts. When I mentioned this to my youngest son, he made a suggestion—Wear a tee shirt over your bathing suit. I wouldn't get sunburned either. Clever kid. Problem solved.

The first cocktail party, strictly for our singles group, was a mad hatters' party. I was amazed at the originality of the hats. People wore huge feathery concoctions and foam creations. The crowd was as diverse as the hats—young, old, fat, thin, and sixty percent women.

The VTG activity director handed out papers covered with squares containing descriptions: lived in the same state as you, loved basketball, born in the same month as you, and traveled to Europe. We were to find different people who could truthfully sign each square.

Feeling insecure, my type-A personality took over. I was one of the first to get all the squares signed, and I won a prize—a Royal Caribbean hot mug. Hmm, food for thought. Do I always go for achievement—my strong suit—when I feel socially inept?

I met Jennifer, a woman from Phoenix who had been active in the chat group, as well as her friend, Marty. I also met two retired Marines, who traded funny stories. A man from Scottsdale snubbed me. He reminded me of one of the beautiful people seen in the "right" Scottsdale bars. Louis, a high school teacher, had a cabin near mine. We talked for a while, and then he followed me around. He was probably feeling anxious too.

We went to dinner and sat at assigned tables. On future nights we could sit at any of the tables designated for our group. I met Ken from Houston. He owned several companies, including an environmental concern whose mission was to spread a product that ate up oil spills. He looked about sixty-five, had white hair, and I could feel good vibes.

Mitch was a lawyer from Ohio, the director of county prisons. Jason was the youngest man in our group, just back from Iraq, a chemist in real life. He was looking to party.

Eric was from a small town in the Midwest and owned a construction company. Right before he left for the cruise, the sheriff of his town called, reporting that Eric's son had been arrested for possession of an open container of liquor in his truck. The kid was too young to legally drink, so Eric talked to the sheriff and the judge and got his son out of jail. He'd have to deal with the rest when he returned home. I could identify with him. What was my son up to in my absence?

After dinner, I returned to my cabin and ate the two chocolate squares on my bed, marveling at the towels folded to look like lions. After resting and watching a basketball game between the Phoenix Suns and the Houston Rockets, I headed to a singles mixer sponsored by the cruise line in the disco on the top deck. I stepped off the elevator and right onto the dance floor. People were dancing, not worrying about being paired off, so I joined in. When I got tired, I went to the bar and bought my favorite beer, Michelob Ultra. A Canadian with a cute accent, gray hair, and a great curly moustache sidled up to me. We danced, and then he kissed me, but we stopped at that.

The next morning at the buffet breakfast, the VTG handlers welcomed us and showed us to our reserved tables. I enjoyed an enlightening conversation with Keith, the businessman I had met at dinner the night before. He'd travelled all over the world. I brought up my proposed "life plan," to sell my car and house when my youngest son moved into his own place, and teach overseas. I mentioned Africa, and he warned me about it, but in terms I hadn't considered before. He said for many people in Africa, life is worth nothing. It's not unusual to see cut-off heads while driving down a road. He said no reason was needed for the taking of a life. His comments made me reconsider the trip to Africa.

At eleven, I took the elevator to the scheduled VTG singles activity in a bar on the top deck. The men and the women met separately to come up with the criteria that we wanted in a date. The women wanted someone financially secure; the men wanted looks. And I had an "aha" moment. The women didn't want to be taken care of by a man; they just wanted to find someone who could carry his own weight financially.

The second activity was called "two truths and a lie." We were to make three statements, one of which was a lie. Our partner would guess the lie. The setup was much like the speed-dating events I'd attended. Women sat in one place and the men spent five minutes with each woman. Since there wasn't any choosing going on, it was a non-threatening way to meet men.

I met Doug from Kansas, who confided in me that he was a millionaire, having sold his farm recently. He said he was looking for a wife. I wasn't going to be any help in that department. I talked with a teacher from California. On the chat line before the cruise, I thought we might click, but it didn't happen.

The rest of the afternoon I read and wrote in my journal on the pool deck.

Our singles game for the next morning was a trivia contest, men vs. women. We had to pick captains. Most of the women pointed at me. Because I was a leader or because I was smart? Something to ponder at another time. The multiple-choice questions were funny. For the men, one question was, "How long should you keep mascara before discarding it?" We won the game.

I had my first date on the cruise. Greg, a guy about my height with a full salt-and-pepper beard, the kind that said, "touch me." Over dinner he told me he was from Texas, divorced, did taxes for Hispanic businesses, and lived in a trailer. It became apparent he'd received the bad financial end of the divorce, but to his credit, he didn't mention it. He seemed a bit shy and wouldn't make a first move. I was feeling uncommonly shy on that front also. A missed opportunity for both of us.

In Key West, I went window shopping, and then returned to the dock to take my tour of the Butterfly Conservatory. A motley assortment of cruisers made up the tour, with only one other person from the singles group, Tom. I told him he reminded me of Roger Moore, and he was flattered. Then I corrected myself to Michael Moore, and he was not at all flattered. Some things are better left unsaid.

I took a zillion pictures of the butterflies as they perched on bushes in a small but well-landscaped garden. When we reached our stop at the aquarium, Tom had vanished. I should have stuck to the Roger Moore comparison.

After dinner, many of us left the ship to join some of the singles group meeting at a local bar, The Lazy Gecko. Eric, the contractor from the Midwest, bought everyone a drink. I talked with him as well as several women and men. We were becoming more comfortable with each other. After two margaritas, the teacher and Joe Bob, the Canadian, walked me back to the ship. They didn't suggest any further activities when we got on board.

I spent some time on a deserted outside deck before I went to the ship's Caribbean Party at the outdoor pool. The steel band's music tickled my ears, and I joined about ten people from our group who formed a circle and danced. The boat's tour director led us in several variants of the electric slide, and we ended with a fun conga line.

The next morning's singles activity was a game of truth or dare. We were divided into co-ed groups, mine being quite jolly. I learned what a wet willie was—the act of licking one's finger and putting it into another person's ear. Yech!

I volunteered to host people for the cabin crawl that afternoon. Joe Bob kindly said he would donate some rum in case I ran out of wine.

Keith suggested we lunch together. As we headed down the stairs for our lunch date, a woman named Caroline—thin, blond, with pale heavy makeup—yelled out to him, "Keith, we need to finish our conversation." She inserted herself between us and even took the seat next to Keith, so he ended up sitting as far as possible from me. Caroline was clearly on a mission to snag him. Oh well.

With plenty of time before the cabin crawl, I met with two women from the singles group to talk about tips for writers. We had a quality discussion, and it felt good to bond with people about a common passion.

I returned to my cabin and opened the Angel Wings wine from the Village of Elgin Winery in Arizona. Tandy and Fritz from across the hall were also hosting. I couldn't quite figure out their relationship. Friends? Body Buddies? Tandy seemed older than he did, though she was in fine shape. She had paid for his part of the trip. They were serving coconut rum with pineapple juice. Who knew coconut rum could be so tasty?

By the time people came through my cabin, I was quite high on the rum. One of the fellows had misbuttoned his loud Hawaiian shirt, so I unbuttoned it and re-buttoned it for him.

Then I got loose lips and made up a secret about the cruise: the Saturday night booty call. We can sleep with whomever we choose because we all get off the ship early the next morning. "Think about it," I said, "If you sleep with someone early in the week, it might get complicated."

One of the men said, "You think like a guy." I didn't know if that was a compliment or not.

Paul snaked his arm around me after that, thinking he had gotten lucky. He said he could make two hours on Friday night the most memorable of my life. Unfortunately, I felt no chemistry or connection.

At the karaoke cocktail party, it was obvious that there were now some "couples." Caroline and Keith were together. Two of the younger members of our group were besotted with each other. The Scottsdale man had potentially found a future trophy wife. We danced while individuals and groups of us sang karaoke with varying degrees of competence.

At dinner the conversation was lively. Everyone over-imbibed the free cocktails, including me. The Canadians cracked up whenever I referred to Joe Bob. Finally, I asked why, and they told me that BOB stood for battery-operated boyfriend. Who knew? He was just Joe after that.

After dinner, I went to the ship's fifties-and-sixties dance. I danced quite a bit, and then returned to my room to gobble my two chocolates and read.

The singles group sponsored only one shore excursion, snorkeling with stingrays in the Grand Caymans. Most of the group had signed up. We took buses and vans to the dock where we boarded large cabin cruisers.

Paul sat next to me and kept talking about Saturday night. I laughed politely, but made no commitment.

We anchored next to other boats at a spot called Sting Ray Alley, and donned our snorkel gear. I was nervous getting in. Would my bathing suit top fall off? But all went well. Until I saw the hordes of stingrays. Those suckers had a diameter of at least four feet, and they were everywhere. I was terrified of stepping on one and getting stung. It took at least ten minutes to conquer that initial fear, then the stingrays seemed like golden retrievers of the sea. I held one. It felt like velvet. I snorkeled again, marveling at fish I'd only seen in pet stores.

Back on the ship, I attended the group's fifties cocktail party. Paul was again hanging around, talking about a sexual feast on Saturday night. He was becoming obnoxious. I kept laughing it off.

I managed to stay away from the hula hoops, but danced instead, freed from the waiting to be asked. Now I could ask a man or a woman to dance with no sexual importance attached.

At the buffet lunch the next day, I met more people from our group and heard the gossip. Big Ernie, the retired mucho macho Marine, had been banned from the formal dining room due to his language and his attempt to extinguish his cigar in a butter dish. I heard that one guy had hooked up with a different woman every night. Another piece of juicy gossip: Last night Caroline stood up and announced that she was going back to her cabin. She waited for a moment, and then said loudly to Keith, "Are you coming?" He was up like a shot and followed her. What else had I missed while reading my book?

After lunch, I changed into my bathing suit and coverup and took the ten-minute taxi ride to the national park. I was excited and nervous about swimming with the dolphins. On the clumsy scale of 1 to 10 with 10 being the clumsiest, I'm a 9. It was possible I'd do something embarrassing.

My disposable underwater camera had malfunctioned, but Sam, another single who was a few inches shorter than I but stocky, promised to bring his. He brought along a baseball cap to cover his balding head, while I wore my pork-pie hat with the strap under my chin. I didn't look in a mirror, wanting to retain my confidence.

Sam wasn't present for the orientation video. He showed up just in time to be assigned to my group. I gingerly stepped along the burning walkway. Why hadn't I remembered to put my water shoes in my bag?

Sam and I had our picture taken with parrots before going to the outdoor pen. Metal mesh enclosed a small part of the ocean. Our group of seven people headed down the stairs and stood on a metal shelf that burned my feet. We were again instructed how to hold our hands and bodies so the dolphins would do the assigned tricks. The videographer and photographer were pointed out, so we could smile in their direction.

It was an amazing experience. I got to pet the two dolphins on their backs and stomachs, kiss one and hold it up by its fins. I took my turn swimming ten yards out to the right position, so the dolphins would come up on each side of me. I grabbed onto their fins and they took me for a ride. Unfortunately, my hat slipped in front of my eyes. Perhaps that heightened the sensory experience.

We each did another trick with the dolphins where they came underneath our feet and pushed us up into the air. It sounded good in theory, but not so good in practice. My feet still burned from standing on the metal mesh shelf, so when the dolphins touched my feet, I flinched instead of relaxing. Instead of springing straight out of the water, I only managed a clumsy splash. Of course, I was the only one without the graceful photo.

We played with the dolphins, splashing them as they circled us. I was feeling high, but became even higher seeing the pure joy on Sam's face when he interacted with the dolphins. He reflected my own wonder and delight.

At dinner I shared the bottle of Arizona wine left over from the cabin crawl. Keith asked me to sit with him, which seemed weird since he and Caroline were a couple. He asked me for my email address, but he never contacted me.

On the last full day, I packed my suitcase, feeling smug that I had managed to wear almost everything I brought. I enjoyed the trip tremendously and didn't want to return home so soon. The people in the singles group were bright, interesting, and for the most part, accepting of one another. My hunch that this would be a fun way for singles to travel proved correct.

The final cocktail party was a Hawaiian luau, and I wore the purple-flowered muumuu I'd bought in Hawaii. Caroline and I chatted, and she told me how she and Keith had flirted via email a few months before the cruise. He recognized her from her photo at the mad hatter cocktail party and called her to task for using a pseudonym on the internet. Then he'd walked away.

She'd searched for him for the first three days of the cruise with no luck. When she saw him on the stairs with me, that's when she said to him, "We need to finish our conversation." Caroline said that they lived only thirty minutes away by plane, so they'd be able to see each other often. He would come to her place or send her a ticket. I knew she wanted him and had snagged him.

I had two powerful piña coladas and told Sam how much I enjoyed swimming with the dolphins with him, and that he had changed my mind about dating short men. I wasn't high enough to share that I was attracted to him. Another missed opportunity. I didn't participate in Saturday night booty call since I didn't feel passionate about any of the guys. My interest in dating and men was waning.

The chat room was left open after the cruise. We shared pictures, memories, and plans. Some people pledged to take the Labor Day Baja cruise. Another group made plans to go to a baseball game in Pittsburgh. A different group planned a trip to Chicago over Labor Day. The most heart-warming part of these plans was that they were open to everyone, not a small clique that had been formed during the cruise.

I met up with some of the Phoenix group at a blues club and another day for lunch. Caroline and Keith got married. I went to a writers' conference with one of the women writers. The cruise was all I had hoped for and more. It was a great venue for a single person who wants to travel, meet people, and have fun. And I gained a new favorite drink, spiced rum and pineapple juice.

After the singles cruise, I went into a dormant period where I didn't date at all. It wasn't that I was angry with men or depressed about rejections or ruled by horniness. I just had too much going on in my life with no time or energy left over for dating.

Chapter Eleven

The Coach

After a two-year hiatus following the cruise, I decided to try dating again. My personal life had calmed down, and I was finally craving some male companionship. I registered on the eHarmony site. After setting up my profile and answering many questions, the site sent me profiles of men matching mine.

I messaged several, but only one guy answered. We made a date to meet at a steak restaurant. I was early; he was on time. The Coach was groomed but appeared older than his sixty-eight years. He was a bit skinny for my taste, but I decided not to let personal appearance play a role in whether I would date a man. Although he was almost bald, he didn't try to cover it up, which I considered a plus.

We talked easily at dinner, and he seemed nice. He had invited me to that restaurant because he had a coupon. I'm not averse to saving money, so that was fine with me. When I shared that fact with some friends, they thought he was cheap. Especially for a first date.

The Coach had been divorced a long time. His grown children lived in the area. He worked as a coffee broker and was the baseball coach at a local junior high school, having been a coach in one form or another most of his adult life. He went to the gym every morning to work out.

I didn't feel chemistry, but I wasn't repulsed. The Coach had some admirable qualities, and he listened as well as talked. Maybe I'd warm up to him. We made a second date when he promised to make dinner for me.

I went to his apartment, a utilitarian place without much decoration except sports trophies. He cooked an excellent fish dinner. He told me he was a writer, too. Poetry. I started to feel the elements react with one another.

The next date was at Eli's to dance. He wanted to dance every number. I wouldn't call him a good dancer, but an aerobic one. By the end of the evening I felt like I'd been to several Zumba sessions, but I'd found a guy who didn't have to down four drinks before getting up to dance. I thoroughly enjoyed the evening.

I let The Coach pick me up at my place for the fourth date. He came with a dozen roses and a poem about how much he liked me. It wasn't good verse, but I appreciated the sentiment and the effort he put into it. It felt good to be adored. I did like him. He had become sexy to me by that time.

We went to bed that night. I found out he had a tiny penis, even when erect. He had the good graces to work hard to satisfy me before he tried insertion. That didn't work well, so I helped him get off.

He coughed a lot that night and got up a couple of times to drink club soda. When I asked him about it, he said he had a lung problem, but didn't want to pollute his body with an inhaler or medicine.

After that, we went out most Saturday nights, either dancing or to the movies. I had a real boyfriend. We were exclusive, and I stopped looking at profiles online. It felt good to be part of a couple again. He told me he loved me. He said it was a shame we hadn't met forty years ago, so we could have had a whole life together. I didn't say "I love you" back. The wall around my heart was high, and he hadn't pierced it yet. The Coach continued to bring me roses every week and write me love poems.

Several months later, I went to Peru for three weeks, one week touring on my own to

Cusco and Machu Pichu, and two weeks in Lima, working in an orphanage on a team from Global Volunteers. We had an Internet connection at the tourist hotel where we stayed, so I posted a journal about my adventure on my blog. I hoped he was reading it.

Although I hadn't pined for The Coach, I missed him a bit. I bought him an alpaca sweater vest. On our first date after my trip, I gave it to him. He took one look at it and gave it back, saying he'd never wear it. My feelings were hurt, but he didn't notice. He told me that he hated picking out presents and always gave gift cards.

I invited him for our family Hanukah celebration, and he met my kids and their families. One night, I met his son and his family. Another night, the Coach and I babysat for his grandsons, five and seven years old. It went well. I was enamored with their huge, friendly golden doodle dog.

One day, he announced he wanted to buy another car because his was getting a bit unreliable. He wanted to shop for one at a dealership in Sun City, which many people did, to find a car that had low mileage and was well-maintained.

I was surprised that he wasn't trading in his ten-year-old Buick. In fact, he was looking for another one just like it. He planned to keep both. I hung around the dealership while he negotiated, then I drove his old car back to his apartment while he drove his "new" old car. That was weird. Two of the same old cars? The Coach never gave me a reasonable answer for buying the same second car.

My childhood friend, who lived in northern California, was turning sixty in February. Her friends were planning a huge party and asked me and another friend from Phoenix to come. They added that The Coach was welcome, too. It was a fun time. The Coach told anyone who would listen that I was the love of his life, and what a wonderful person I was. I felt terrific to be surrounded by this flattery.

Later in February, he asked if he could use my copy of TurboTax to do his taxes. I agreed. He fed me the information and I entered it. I was shocked to see how little he made and how small his investments were.

The Coach wanted to go on a short vacation to San Diego, so I found great deals on a hotel and flights. He wanted to go to Sea World, The San Diego Zoo, and the Safari Park Zoo; he wasn't interested in any cultural events or the beach, my favorite destinations in California.

We drove our rental car to a cove in La Jolla and watched the seals. I took lots of photos. I loved taking pictures of animals, so I knew I'd enjoy this vacation. The next day we went to the zoo, and I was shocked at how many times he had to stop to rest. He complained that the humidity was aggravating his respiratory condition, which he treated with club soda. The guy went to the gym every day. Didn't that build up stamina? I had no problem with my stamina.

The Coach was exhausted after our day and didn't want to go anywhere but dinner in our hotel. I was worried about his fatigue and asked him if he needed medical attention, but he brushed off my concerns.

During the next few days, we visited the Safari Park and Sea World. I had a great time and captured some wonderful photos of the animals. They would make an excellent animal book for my granddaughter.

The Coach was looking more and more tired every day. We ate at the same hotel restaurant every evening and kept to our room at night. I asked him several times if he needed to see a doctor, but he pushed my concerns aside.

We returned home on a Monday. The Coach called me on Friday to say that he wouldn't be coming over the following evening. In fact, he wouldn't be seeing me again. We were too different, he said. He hadn't been to the gym in a while and had seen more movies in the last nine months than he had in his life. I led a sedentary life, and he was more active. In shock, I didn't argue. I just said a quick "good bye" and hung up.

After the shock wore off, I got angry. I couldn't believe it. This guy had told anyone who would listen that I was the most wonderful person he'd ever met, and I was the love of his life. I hadn't stopped him from going to the gym, except maybe on Sundays, when he stayed over. Why had he broken up with me? Just as I was beginning to trust a man again, he pulled the rug out. I felt emotionally betrayed. What about the weekly roses? What about the love poems? This reminded me how poorly I read people.

I fumed but realized I wasn't crushed. I hadn't loved *him*. I loved being part of a couple again.

A friend assured me The Coach would recognize his mistake and want to continue the relationship. Sure enough, several months later he called me to tell me he wanted to get back together. He made some lame excuse that he had broken up with me to make time to help one of his sons, who needed emotional support. That didn't fly with me. I told him that if he'd been honest, I would have agreed to stop seeing each other until his son was better. Then I said that I felt emotionally betrayed and I wouldn't see him again.

He wrote me a letter a few months after that, asking me to go out with him when I returned to Scottsdale in the fall. I didn't answer the letter. I was done with him.

Lesson learned: The old man, the old car—read the signals.

Chapter Twelve
The Widower

I bought a small cabin in the town of Munds Park, about twenty miles south of Flagstaff, Arizona, where it's thirty degrees cooler due to the elevation. The older I got, the more the Phoenix summers bother me. Munds Park was a mostly white, "coupled" society, both straight and gay. There are about three thousand homes in the town, but most are used as second homes. That first summer I didn't dating at all, settling in and communing with nature.

The second summer after The Coach dumped me, I lost some weight and was feeling more confident. I decided to try dating in the Flagstaff area and joined Plenty of Fish, a free site. A fellow, whose photo made him look like a movie star, emailed me immediately about meeting me. A retired widower, he was looking for someone with whom to enjoy his life. He lived in Sedona, but he was willing to drive to Flagstaff to meet at Starbuck's.

I was early. As soon as he exited his car, I recognized him. He was as good-looking as his photo. A warm smile lit up his face. We took our drinks to a table apart from the people huddled over their laptops and tablets.

He told me that his wife had been ill for several years. They were preparing to divorce when she became ill. Under the circumstances, he didn't want to care for her, but he paid for home care. That seemed a bit hard-hearted to me, but I couldn't judge since I didn't know all the facts. She died a year ago. Afterward, he pulled up stakes and moved from cold Minnesota to the warmth of Sedona.

The Widower asked me questions and listened carefully to my answers. Sometimes he asked me to clarify something—a great listener, unlike many other first dates I'd had.

After an hour and a half, he asked me to go to dinner with him at a nearby restaurant. I accepted, and we continued our conversation. I was smitten. He was charming, interesting, and accepting. The Widower said he felt we had something special going, just what he was looking for, a long-term relationship. I wasn't as thrilled with this statement, not interested in a lifetime or even long-term commitment.

He walked me to my car and gave me a passionate kiss, which I returned. He asked if he could visit me in Munds Park. I agreed, and we set a date for later in the week.

When I arrived home, I found a message from another man in Sedona who wanted to meet me. Although smitten with The Widower, I made a date with the new man for the following week in Sedona.

The Widower came over later that week. I served wine and we talked. Then he came on strong—aggressive even. I was no virgin, but something about his manner sounded an alarm. I pushed him off. He got up and ranted that I was a tease and stormed out.

This turn of events dumbfounded me. He had seemed so nice and interested in me. I couldn't believe how bad I was at understanding men. I talked to a few women who used dating sites and they filled me in. "Players" trolled dating websites, looking for new women. Figuring they were lonely, the trolls made a date and pitched long-term commitments. They pushed for sex early on. If the women wasn't ready, the Players dropped the women. If the women did go to bed, they also dropped the women, another notch on his bedpost.

I was glad I'd rescued myself and was ever afterward on the lookout for "players." Lesson learned: A movie star-looking date might just be a troll.

Chapter Thirteen
Mr. Spiritual Journey

I met Mr. Spiritual Journey at a coffee shop in The Village of Oak Creek, just south of Sedona. He sported a lot of wavy light brown hair and a twinkle in his eyes. Tall, he outweighed me, though not fat, just well-built.

Mr. Spiritual Journey had owned a construction company but sold it five years before to retire at fifty-five. He moved to Sedona to enrich his spiritual life. Divorced for many years, he had a daughter and granddaughter who lived in Mesa, Arizona. He advocated a healthy lifestyle but wasn't a fanatic. The man meditated for an hour every morning, followed by an hour of Tai Chi, followed by a hike in the red rocks. I admired his perseverance toward his goal, not to mention his looks and personality.

We made another date to go dancing in Sedona. Although it's only thirteen miles from Munds Park as the crow flies, it takes fifty minutes by road. I was willing to drive that far and back to see him again.

We ate at a Szechuan restaurant with an outside patio facing the Red Rocks. The Chinese food was the best I'd tasted in northern Arizona. Then we went to a local club. I was pleased that he didn't need to be liquored up to dance. The band was happening, the atmosphere pulsed, and I was a dancing fool. I felt comfortable in his arms when we slow-danced.

We went back to his place, a large modular home in a rural neighborhood. The porch had a gorgeous view of the Red Rocks of Sedona. We sipped wine out there. He was an experienced lover, and I enjoyed the sex.

We dated a lot that summer, mostly in Sedona. Since I was a member of the Sedona International Film Society, which showed independent films in their own theater, we attended several of their offerings and I delighted in our spirited conversations about the movies.

Mr. Spiritual Journey took me to Wet Beaver Creek. I am a linear thinker and totally goal-oriented. Mr. Spiritual Journey was the opposite, since the journey was the *raison d'être.* We were sitting at a picnic bench in the shade when he asked me about my spiritual beliefs. He had to coax it out of me since I spent little time thinking in that dimension. After an hour or so, we finally found some common ideas and vocabulary. He then went over breathing, what to expect, no time limits, and how to watch the parade of thoughts without latching onto any.

We used the Porta Potties before we hiked the short way to the creek. I loved the exposed, gnarled roots of an old tree. Mr. Spiritual Journey spread a blanket on the red rocks in the middle of the creek and we meditated. He told me to stir when I was done so he would come out of his meditation.

It worked. Meditation transported me from my worries, and I had no trouble shutting out worldly thoughts. Afterwards, we munched on fruit and talked about the experience. Yet the tranquil setting was getting a bit hot for me. It's at least fifteen degrees warmer in Sedona than Munds Park, especially in the sun. We rearranged our positions and I chose to put my feet in the chilly creek before we meditated again. I transported even deeper into it and stopped feeling my feet in the water. Mr. Spiritual Journey said I had experienced an out-of-body experience, but I wasn't not into that interpretation. After that day, he found lovely spots for us to meditate. He went to group mediations, but he didn't invite me to go with him. I wondered why.

We went to Dancing on the Square in Flagstaff and tried out salsa steps. I had no great designs for a future with him, although we had two great summers of romance. Until the day he came to my cabin. After satisfying sex, we discussed philosophy. We had spoken of deep subjects before, specifically the existence of God. He had extolled the Spirit, but I wasn't convinced of an overriding force. My spiritual beliefs tended toward the idea that the world was chaos, and we created our own meaning of it.

He was also into transmigration of souls. "Everything happens for a reason," he assured me. "We come back to learn lessons from our previous lives."

That didn't work for me. "What would be the reason that my daughters, ages seven and thirteen, were killed in a commercial airline flight?"

"It happened because there was a lesson you needed to learn from it," he said.

His answer hit me in the gut. Appalled at the notion that my sweet darlings were killed because of a mistake I made in a prior life, I couldn't accept it. I certainly had grown from the experience. It's something I'll never get over, but have learned to live with it.

Every time he answered my questions, he dug himself into a deeper hole. His comments held the opposite of empathy. He gazed at me with pity because I couldn't reach his level of enlightenment.

I suppressed my anger. No matter how much I argued with him, he wouldn't change his point of view. He had read and studied Buddhism enough to be dangerous without being enlightened.

As he left, we made no definite plans to see each other.

And we didn't.

Lesson learned: Beware enlightened men of any sort.

Chapter Fourteen
More One Date Wonders

After returning to Scottsdale in the fall, I monitored my messages on Match.com and Plenty of Fish. They yielded more one-date wonders.

Mr. Criminal

One fellow emailed me and asked for my phone number. The first time he called, I was at the beach in California with my kids. He said he would call the next day but didn't. No big deal.

The second time he called, he seemed surprised that I answered. He said he just wanted to leave a message and that he would call later in the day. He didn't. What was up with this guy?

The third time he called, we talked for a while and decided to meet at a Starbuck's at Desert Ridge after I dined with my oldest son and his family. My profile pictures posted on my profile were recent so I figured even if he didn't resemble his, we'd find each other.

I arrived at Starbuck's right on time. As he approached, I noted that he appeared just like his picture, not handsome but interesting. He bought me a large iced tea and we chatted. He mostly talked about his business and raising his daughter in a rural area, so she could have ponies, peacocks, sheep, goats, dogs, cats, and horses. We laughed about both growing up in New Jersey, and I figured I'd see him again. He suggested we trade services. I would write copy for his website and he would have someone lay the tile in my living room. He kissed me at my car, a good kiss. I was feeling hopeful.

Before I climbed in the car, he said, "You'll probably Google me as soon as you get home, so I want to let you know what you'll find. Forty years ago, I was involved with some fake money." He handed me his card.

I wouldn't have been able to Google him because I didn't know his last name, but he had just provided it. "Forty years ago is a long time," I said brightly.

"Also," he said, "a guy I recently stopped being partners with has a blog. Don't believe what he writes."

"Okay," I said.

I got in my car and drove home. This was a bit weird.

The next day I was leaving for a vacation to San Francisco. Waiting for the plane to board, I Googled him. I read about the counterfeit money case. He'd failed to mention his extensive criminal record. So, it wasn't just a one-time thing. He was a voluntary witness—informant—for the prosecution against Giuliano. The mob family?

The blog was listed next, but I didn't go there. Of interest was a recent appellate-court opinion. The judge wrote that the fellow I'd just met was the defendant in a fraud case involving mortgages. He and a loan officer conspired to allow investors to buy rental properties without any down payment.

Having lost a lot of money in the two businesses I funded for my second husband, I was uncomfortable knowing that he sometimes leaned over the ethical line. This new guy hadn't just leaned over the line; he'd jumped to the other side. Obviously, I wasn't not good at parsing out bad characters on a first date. I thought he was intriguing, not a member of the mob.

I was going to call to inform him there would be no second date but emailed instead through the dating website. All he had was my cell phone number but no last name, no address. I wrote a short note that the counterfeit money and the blog were not the reasons I wouldn't see him, but the fraud case troubled me. I wished him good luck in the future.

He emailed back a lame explanation that he was an unwitting party. I didn't think so. That was the end of our conversation. Whew! Dodged that one.

Mr. No-Show

I made a date with a fellow who lived on the west side of town. We agreed to meet at a Barnes and Noble café in the geographic middle. He had been emailing me about his adventures on a trip to visit relatives that turned him into a cupcake baker for a few days. I was anxious to hear about it. Then he called to change the plans. Then he wrote to say he had cancelled something else, so it was okay.

I put on makeup and chose my outfit carefully. Arriving a few minutes early, I ordered a large hot tea. At ten, I got a phone call from Mr. No Show. His car wouldn't start. That was ridiculous because he would have had to start out at nine-thirty to make it to our meeting. I didn't rant, but rather stewed as I sat at a table, finishing my hot tea. I realized I should have said something and not swallowed my annoyance. I had the feeling he came to the café, peeked at me, and decided against meeting me. Or he was married.

In any case, he hasn't called or emailed, so another one bit the dust.

Chapter Fifteen
Mr. Mistaken Identity

I spent the day with the grandkids—baking cookies, finishing presents, and going to the theater to see *Junie B. Jones: Jingle Bells, Batman Smells.* We had a good time, but I was ready to deliver the kids home in the late afternoon.

Many messages awaited from different guys on a dating website that day. The emails seem to go in cycles. There are weeks when no one's interested, and weeks when I'm a hot prospect. I have no idea why. As I've stated before, I'm reactive, not proactive on the dating website since I hardly ever go looking for guys to date. I wait until someone emails me. It says something about me, but I'm not sure what. I guess I'm the opposite of desperate.

One of the fellows wanted to meet that night. What the heck, I could use a cocktail and some adult company. I agreed to meet him at Eddie's House, a favorite place of mine for happy hour. After hurrying home to put on makeup and change clothes, I called him to say I was on the way. He said he was already there.

One single guy sat at the bar. I smiled at him, and said "hi." He smiled back, so I sat down next to him. I asked him what he was drinking, and he said vodka and grapefruit juice. Not my thing. I ordered a lemon drop. He asked the bartender where his flatbread was, and I was surprised he'd already ordered.

He didn't look anything like the picture from the website, but that's not unusual. More like Kirk Douglas, the old version. He barely gave me a chance to speak. He went on and on about his farms in Nebraska, his place in Prescott on the Arnold Palmer golf course, and his home in Costa Rica.

The good-looking fellow sitting a few seats down the bar seemed more interesting.

When my date's flatbread arrived, he didn't offer me any. I knew I'd never date the guy again. I ordered my own happy hour food, a steak quesadilla. He babbled on about big shots he knew. When he asked for the check, the bartender asked me if I wanted mine. I agreed, glad to get away from the guy.

I paid, then took out my phone, which listed quite a few calls from the fellow I was supposed to meet. How was that possible when I was sitting right next to him? I called him back, curious. A guy answered—definitely not the person I'd been talking to. I glanced at the other man at the bar, who held a phone to his ear.

I hung up and moved next to him. He had stood outside the door for twenty minutes waiting for me and figured I had stood him up. I was so embarrassed I wanted to melt into the barstool.

He was a good sport about it and we laughed. He had already made another "meet and greet," since he thought I stood him up. I'm sure he'll never call me, and I don't blame him.

Lesson learned: Confirm that I'm speaking to the right person.

Chapter Sixteen
Mr. Mechanical Ability

I finally bought a barbeque grill. First, I should admit I'm afraid of fire. The gas or charcoal grills I owned before were the husbands' domains. Over the past few years, I'd been on the lookout for a new grill, but never found one worth buying. They all seemed like George Foreman grills on steroids.

I was in Scottsdale Fashion Square when I passed a display of grills next to a kiosk. They were electric, but they used wood pellets which caught on fire and cooked the food. The salesman said the grill was a barbecue, smoker, and a convection oven. He was a good salesman, but I didn't understand how the thing worked. The man assured me it was simple to assemble. Famous last words.

The salesman loaded it into the back seat of my compact car. At home, I had trouble getting it out of the car because the box was heavy. The man must have had herculean strength to heft it in so easily. I removed some of the pieces until the box was light enough for me to lift.

I possess many kinds of intelligences. Mechanical ability is not one of them, so I called and texted my middle son, the one who is gifted in that area, but got no reply. I took the grill out of the box and stared at the pieces, totally intimidated.

A few nights later, I had a first date with a guy who didn't drink alcohol or coffee. I suggested we meet at The Sugar Bowl, an ice cream parlor in downtown Scottsdale. I arrived early but had a hard time finding a parking space. It was during spring training, and downtown Scottsdale was filled with throngs of people day and night.

The hostess seated me, and I waited, playing the Scrabble game on my phone.

My date came to my table. He was quite good looking, and he laid on the flattery. But his eyebrows rose when I ordered a regular, not a small, sundae.

You are not my diet master.

He proceeded to expound on random work stories from the past. I guess he thought they painted him in a good light, but I didn't think so. Mr. Mechanical Ability had worked on a cattle farm somewhere in Arizona and managed to clean up the water supply and get an underling to spit polish the barns. His boss took the credit for it, and that pissed him off.

Sex and the Single Senior

He also worked on a dairy farm in Utah and spied on some workers who were ripping off the owner. He came off as holier-than-thou. I also got the drift that he was currently unemployed.

Mr. Mechanical Ability explained that he cheated on his wife because they hadn't been intimate for two years. To me, adultery was a chicken's way out of a marriage. I spoke from experience. That's what both of my husbands did. Why not have the gumption to talk to your spouse? He also divulged juicy gossip about some dates he'd been on. Not nice.

Finally we reached the part of the conversation when he asked what I was looking for in a relationship.

"Fun and a companion," I said. "What about you?"

He shrugged. "I just want someone there when I come home at night."

"That's nice. Maybe if I had someone like that, my new barbecue wouldn't be lying in pieces at home."

"I could put it together for you. How about tomorrow?"

I brightened. "Sure, that would be great."

"Why don't you check the instructions and email me what tools to bring." He walked me to my car, parked on a nearby street. After I climbed in, he leaned in and kissed me once, then dove in for a wet one. I was not going to make out in the middle of crowds in downtown Scottsdale. Nonplussed, I drove away.

Later as I sat in my kitchen, sipping a soda, I thought about his conversation. He wasn't someone I wanted to date. Pompous, unemployed, a cheater, and probably a player. Glad I hadn't given him my address, I texted him that I thought over our conversation and we weren't a match because he wanted someone 24/7 and I would never.be that person. I felt enormous relief.

After all that, I didn't need a date to put my BBQ together. My son, who lives on the other side of the valley, called me back, came over and put the BB together in a half an hour.

And my son was much better company. Lesson learned: I don't need a man to fix things. I have sons and a handyman for that.

Chapter Seventeen
Mr. Liberal Democrat

I had a coffee/tea date with a guy who's a liberal Democrat. That's a miracle in Arizona, a red state—the home of Barry Goldwater and John McCain. I'm an old-style liberal. We talked about national and Arizona politics, health-care reform, our families and work. And we had chemistry. At the end of a lovely evening, we kissed.

Light at heart, I drove home. Although I tell myself each time I meet a nice guy with whom I have chemistry, *take it easy*, I always find myself imagining possible future dates of dancing, movies, kissing, and reading the paper together.

That night I woke up feeling sick. The eruptions from all orifices started and lasted five hours. No need to chronicle this, but I took at least four showers and cleaned my tile floors several times. These are the times I'm glad I'm single. How humiliating to spew in front of someone else. How ignominious to have no control over bodily functions.

I felt duty-bound to text Mr. Liberal Democrat (MLD) about what he might have contracted. Still, he emailed me back and we made a date. Luckily, he didn't get the stomach bug I had, or I might never have heard from him again.

For our second date, we went to The Compound and listened to a jazz quartet. The talk reached a more personal and soul-bearing level. I told him about my daughters and he told me about his failed marriage and that he'd messed up three relationships, each after ninety days. Should I start marking the days off on a calendar?

Our third date was dinner at Humble Pie. You gotta love a guy who likes clams on his pizza. . We felt good enough about each other that we planned three more dates.

My friend came in for the holidays. It was good that we didn't see each other for a week. My new romance was heating up fast, which was scary for me, since I was still so naïve. I believed everything MLD said about himself. I didn't want to repeat the experience of being with a player who cut me off after going to bed with him. Yet a part of me yearned for the old mores of the sexual revolution, the ones I experienced between my two marriages. Then I didn't have to count the dates or weeks before jumping into bed with a hot man. How did these days get to be so conservative? I guess it was during the fifteen years I was married the second time.

After my friend left, I saw MLD again. We had a talk about expectations. He told me he was looking for his "one true love, the only one in the world for him." and he said I wasn't the one. That stung. I told him to stay honest and let me know when we were no longer an exclusive item, or he wanted to date other people. He assured me he enjoyed my company and wasn't looking for someone else for the time being.

One morning a few weeks later, after I'd spent the night at his home, he asked me if I wanted an omelet like the one he'd made me last week. The problem was—he hadn't made me an omelet last week. Was he seeing someone else or had he forgotten I wasn't hungry last week?

It was so much easier to keep everything straight when we were younger because our memories were better. Now it was harder to remember who did what. I was an optimist to think this way. Was this a warning sign? Or was it a senior mistake and I should give the man some slack? I decided not to make a big deal about it. One cannot underestimate the power of regular sex from a source other than Mr. Buzzy, my vibrator. I liked the feel of MLD's arms around me and his body near me when I slept.

I went out with MLD for a dinner and a concert by Robben Ford, a jazz guitarist who branched out to the blues and rock.

MLD had told me that he didn't dance unless he'd had some beers. I offered to be the designated driver and he accepted. When we arrived at The Compound, a now-defunct venue in North Scottsdale, we were given wrist bands and set loose. The show was supposed to start at eight. We arrived a little after seven, yet no empty tables remained. We asked a couple if we could share their table and they readily agreed. Thomas and Diane were a delightful pair who had been together for almost forty years.

At eight, it was announced that the show was a sellout and would start at nine. A few minutes later the staff made everyone give up their chairs and tables to clear the floor.

Thomas and Diane went to stand by the bandstand and we followed. By this time, the crowd that curled around the building was allowed in from the cold. The staff never brought back any chairs and expected us to stand.

The burgeoning crowd was eighty percent men. I mentioned this to Diane, and she said that the people who attended concerts like this were guitar geeks, like her husband.

The band started about quarter after nine and played for two hours. I enjoyed the music. It was rocking, and MLD and I danced in place. I surveyed the room and saw that only one other person, a woman, was making any kind of dancing moves. A few of the men were doing the head-shaking thing, but most were still. It must be true that most guys don't like to dance. Here was a big room of musicians, and no one was bopping out.

I attended a Los Lobos concert with Mr. Liberal Democrat at the same venue. The first show had sold out, so we went to the eleven o'clock late show, a bit worried about staying up. That concern reminded me that we no longer were kids, who start their evening at eleven.

The crowd was mixed but tended toward senior citizens, since Los Lobos has been around for thirty years. We were seated next to a table of three women who were a bit older than we were. Their hairstyles were French twists with teasing on the top. They were weekly-beauty-shop ladies. During the concert, they danced around in their seats. Most of the audience got on the dance floor—singles, couples, everyone. Were these women held back from doing this because they were brought up during a time when women had to wait for men to ask them before they ventured out on a public dance floor? I had no such inhibitions. Los Lobos played "La Bamba" at the end of the concert. I went on stage with four other women and danced with the band.

Do I have fewer inhibitions as I age? Thirty years ago, I wouldn't have jumped on stage. When I was younger, I was more self-conscious about my body. I thought it had to be perfect. Now that everything is yielding to gravity, I am less inhibited, and I am unwilling to pay to make it look younger. I do work out, but it doesn't stop the aging process. When I look at the old pictures of me in a bathing suit, I can't understand why I was so obsessed with comparing myself to perfect bodies. Mu body was darned good. Too bad I didn't appreciate it. Now I can get changed in a locker room without hiding my body or constantly comparing it to other women's.

Sex is less restrained. None of us are virgins. We seniors don't have to worry about getting pregnant or whether others think we're easy. However, STD's and AIDS still must be considered.

An artist friend sent me an email invitation to an open-studio event near downtown Phoenix. I wanted to go but wouldn't make the effort by myself. Since I had a date with MLD to go to the Rhythm

Room, not far from the artist's studio, he agreed to combine the two events. The art part of my brain was stimulated by the different artists and their works at the studio. The music-and-dance part of my brain was in overdrive listening and dancing to the music of the Sugar Thieves, a favorite local band. I realized if I hadn't been dating, I would have missed out on both these events I enjoyed immensely.

One Saturday, I played nine holes of golf with Mr. Liberal Democrat. I liked to play golf, but never found the time or person with whom to do so. I had a fantastic time. He wasn't competitive, didn't count strokes, was better than I, and enjoyed the ambiance of a golf course and the fun of the game.

So that's why I date. For me, the companionship, fun, and intimacy were worth rejection and the occasional heartache.

Everyone remembers my birthday because it's on St. Patrick's Day. For my sixty-first birthday, I went to an Irish bar with a group of friends and MLD. I hadn't been out for St Patrick's Day in many years. The Sugar Thieves played while I drank much more than I had for decades. Mr. Liberal Democrat agreed to be the designated driver.

MLD's ninety-day expiration date was two days after my birthday. When we passed that milestone, I thought the curse had been lifted. But I saw the signs—things weren't quite right.

For the past month, we hadn't gone out on Saturday nights. My sister, the dating queen, informed me that meant he was in a relationship with someone else. He texted less often. When I asked him if there was a problem, he said he was having a hard time at work and told me about it. I felt like the girlfriend whining for attention. The next week, he seemed distracted. I asked about that. He said he was having personal problems and might start seeing a counselor.

The relationship reached a breaking point. He neither called, emailed, nor texted me during the next week. When I texted whether we'd go out on the weekend, he didn't respond. I knew he wasn't a person who liked to plan. I, on the other hand, plan everything. After no word from him Thursday, I texted, "You okay?" but received no response.

He broke up with me with silence. *Ghosted*—that was a new one for me. I thought it made him a chicken. In my set of dating etiquette, if you'd had a relationship with someone for almost four months, an in-person talk was required.

I retreated to my woman cave and pondered what part of the failure of the relationship was mine. Was I too nice again?

Did I exude a clingy message? I didn't want a years-long commitment, but would like an exclusive relationship while it lasts. Is that an oxymoron?
Lesson Learned: Pay attention to signs a man gives you.

Chapter Eighteen
The Perpetual Student

I sought comfort in my cabin in northern Arizona and found a fellow to date. He was sixty-three and still had a semester before he earned his bachelor's degree at Northern Arizona University. He'd been laid off a few years before and decided to take out student loans and go back to college.

We had some great discussions, but he tended to lecture on what he was learning in class. After a month or two, this was tedious. He was especially into "mindfulness." I know there have been terrific results with this philosophy, but I wasn't into it.

The Perpetual Student was applying to graduate school and trying to get a grant or loan for it. He didn't mind living like a student. I admired his asceticism but didn't share it. Question: If he finished his master's degree at sixty-five or so, how was he going to pay back his loans on a counselor's or social worker's salary?

I knew he'd been married, but he never mentioned his ex-wife. That was fine with
me.

When we finally did go to bed, he was again "the instructor." It wasn't romantic or
passionate. After that, he became more smitten with me as I tired of him.

I decided to break up with him. It was hard to do kindly and politely, but I tried. It wasn't fair to tell him by text, phone or email that the relationship was not going to blossom into a romance, but I needed to tell him soon.

Even though he was a handsome guy and happy with himself, I didn't feel any emotional connection. Rejection isn't fun, even if you've been together for only a few months. It was the first time in a while that I was the "breaker." Certainly, I'd told fellows I'd met that there wouldn't be a second date, but this was different. We'd shared some life stories.

I asked him to meet me. He chose a place where I could have tea and he could
have a glass of wine. It didn't appear that he had any idea why I wanted to meet. The Perpetual Student was probably hoping he'd get lucky. We talked for about a half an hour before I brought up my reason for meeting. I

told him that he was a great guy, handsome and interesting, but not for me.

He slumped in his seat. and asked me what I was looking for. When I said I wasn't sure, he said that was a common response. I owned up that I wanted a strong emotional connection. He peered at me quizzically. He said he thought we had an emotional bond. Awkward.

He wanted to know if he was undesirable because of his lack of money. Since I had been looking for a summer romance, I honestly told him that was not the case.

I decided to make it a clean break. He suggested "friends with benefits" but I said no. I was flattered that he thought I was desirable, but at that time I was looking for a meaningful, if transitory, relationship.

He finished his wine and I finished my tea. He walked me back to my car and told me it was the nicest breakup he'd ever experienced. That made me feel better and confirmed my methodology.

Lesson learned: There are good ways to break up.

Chapter Nineteen
The Train Man Stops at My Station the First Time

After The Perpetual Student, I decided to take another chance. I met Train Man. He was an engineer, the person who drives the train. His freight train went from Winslow, Arizona to Needles, California. Although his schedule varied every week, he had two days on and two days off, but the departures and arrivals were different every trip. This was a challenge for a person like me who liked to plan everything in advance. I never knew what days I was going to see him. It didn't hurt his case that he was handsome, liked to listen to live music and dance, was politically liberal, and listened to National Public Radio.

Train Man was a doer. One day we took his truck on an off-road vehicle trip down Schnebly Hill to Sedona and picnicked by a swimming hole on Beaver Creek. Another day we visited the V Bar V Ranch National Park, which was famous for petroglyphs. On another jaunt, we got to see the bison at Mormon Lake, passing by both Upper and Lower St. Mary's Lake.

Train Man joined me for happy hour at Pinewood Country Club. We drove through Bearizona and attended the bird show there. We danced at the country club to a live band. On several occasions, we went to Charley's in the Wetherford Hotel to listen to the Monday Night Blues Band. I had to pick him up those nights since he couldn't risk drinking anything and driving. He'd lose his job.

Train Man planned most of the outings. I let him know that being a willing follower was not a usual part of my personality. In past relationships, I'd been the one to do most of the planning, but it was relaxing to sit back and let someone else do it. However, I hoped he hadn't gotten the impression that I was a docile woman. Then again, we'd spent enough time together for him to see my assertive side.

The sex was excellent. His member was not inordinately long, but it had width that made it quite exciting. Sometimes we made love in the forest.

These were the things I liked about him:

- He loved to listen to live music and dance.

- He thought dancing with my single friends was a hoot, not a burden.

- His children and grandchildren were his top priority.

- I liked his looks and sturdy body type.

- He was a liberal union member.

- He had an optimistic outlook on life.

- He'd also lost a child, so he understood me.

So why did we stop seeing each other after a few months that summer? I texted and called, but received no reply. Disappointed but not heartbroken, I realized it was fun, and just a summer romance.

Lesson learned: Don't get upset over summer flings.

Chapter Twenty
Mr. Missed Chance

I went into puberty in the sixties and was part of the women's movement. I believed in sexual freedom even though I didn't practice it then. When I married in 1970, I was a virgin.

During my first single-again experience in the early eighties, after my first divorce, I finally got to fool around a bit, but not on a large scale. Now that I was single again for the second time, the Doris Day, good girl/bad girl dilemma, reared its head.

When I moved back to my home in Scottsdale from my summer cabin in the mountains, I tried again to find a fellow to date. Remember Scrabble Man's unwritten rule that you could have sex on the third date? I should have listened to him.

I used to get an email every week from Dr. Cupid, a guy who sponsored singles dances, which he called "Calculated Couples." One night the dance was held at a resort near my home.

More women attended than men, as usual. I felt as uncomfortable as ever, like I did during junior high dances. After a tour around the room, I stood by the wall and noticed a guy who appealed to me. He was about six feet tall with a medium build, balding with white hair, glasses, and a kind and gentle "grandpa" face. He wore a golf shirt and khaki pants.

I grabbed a glass of club soda with lemon and eased my way over to him. We started to talk and we clicked. I could feel the chemistry rising the first time we danced a slow dance. We danced some more, and we talked. Later, when the ballroom was almost deserted, we strolled to the resort pool and kissed in the shadows. It was romantic. I wanted to rip his clothes off right then, but it was too soon. He took my phone number.

Mr. Missed Chance called the next day and we chatted. He called again a few days later to invite me over for steak and to sort his wife's books—she had died five months before. Since I was a librarian, it was my forte. He had sold his home and was moving at the end of the month.

Excited to see him again, I drove to his home in Scottsdale and was pronounced "okay" by his dog, Nada. He smoked a cigar on the patio while he grilled us marinated portobello mushrooms and steak on an old-fashioned Weber barbeque. We conversed about children, work, retirement, and laughed at each other's anecdotes.

After dinner, we went into the library to begin sorting the books. He had already told me he read little fiction, so I knew the left bookshelf was hers because it was filled with poetry and murder mysteries. His bookshelf on the right was lined with books about baseball, cigars, golf, and photography. It didn't take me long to figure out the few books he might want from her side—misfiled non-fiction books and ones she'd had inscribed for him.

I suggested that he take the unwanted books to a public library where they would either add them to the collection or sell them in the library's bookstore for funds to support programs. He thanked me for helping him sort through the books, and then he kissed me. I thought he was ready. We were both hot for each other, and I figured we'd make out, and then I'd go home.

Unfortunately, it had been a while since I'd had any intimate contact. He ignited a fire I couldn't douse. We ended up in the bedroom, unclothed and devouring each other. I asked if he had a condom. He didn't. He said he hadn't expected us to get into bed. I was mortified. Not only did I not come prepared, but this told me we'd had the same expectations for the evening. We didn't have intercourse, but oral sex.

Mr. Missed Chance called me a few times after that, but the conversations were cool. We never went out again. He was still in the mourning period for his wife, but his sex drive wasn't. His heart and his brain weren't ready for someone new. Lover's remorse. I ruined what could have been a good thing by jumping into physical intimacy too soon. It was a lesson learned the hard way.

So here was the paradox: how to be a vixen in bed and a nice girl too.

Lesson learned: Scrabble Man was right.

Chapter Twenty-One
The Roadie

A year later, I emailed a fellow in Scottsdale a few times and he suggested meeting at a British pub I'd never heard of. I was horny as I hadn't had any sex for a year, so I wore a black tee shirt that showed cleavage. I usually don't do this, but I wanted to look hot.

As soon as he spoke, I knew why he'd picked the pub. He was English. I'm a sucker for an accent. He had been a roadie sound man for twenty years, with bands like Santana, Wings, and U2. I was impressed and loved his anecdotes.

He told me that Santana insisted everyone on his tour have a will. If they didn't, Santana's lawyer drew one up for them. And he hung out with Paul McCartney in English pubs when he worked on the Wings tour.

Now the Roadie worked for a Native American tribe as the stage manager for both of their casino showrooms. He invited me to have dinner at his place the next week. I usually don't do that, but as I said, I was horny.

He lived in a modular home in a trailer court in Scottsdale. The Roadie's home was tidy and he had a kick-ass sound system. Of course, he was the sound guy on the road. He had an exceptional LP collection and played whatever I chose.

The Roadie made what I discovered was a traditional English dinner—peas, mashed potatoes from scratch and pork chops. Everything was tasty. He'd been honest about being a good cook.

After dinner, we made out on the living room couch, listening to vinyl records. When things got hot and heavy, he excused himself to do something in the bathroom. He told me he had to give himself a shot to help with an erection. Casanova had to do the same thing. Did they inject their penises? I'm glad they never asked me to do it. In my experience, most men over sixty either take pills or inject themselves. We returned to the living room to talk and neck. When he felt ready, we moved into his bedroom.

He was good in bed, as was I—total satisfaction all the way around.

I developed a liaison with The Roadie. I saw him weekly for about nine months. We never went out. I'd go over to his place, we told each other amusing anecdotes from our lives, he cooked dinner for me, and we ended up in bed. It wasn't a relationship, in that I didn't think of him when we weren't together, and I doubt he thought about me. We had fun and *naughty*—his word—times together.

The Roadie was an interesting fellow. We shared some of our family stories and each week we reviewed what was new. He cooked me dinner—steak, pork chops, Beef Bourguignon, stew, and mashed potatoes made from scratch.

I realized that men who are comfortable financially rarely go on dating sites unless they're players—men looking to sleep with as many women as possible. The Roadie alluded to his tight finances. I assumed that's why we never went out anywhere. He promised me tickets for shows at the casino, but they never materialized.

I did see him at work one time. Cheech and Chong were playing at one of the casino showrooms he managed. A friend and I bought tickets to see them. I had just had some vein surgery, so one of my legs was mummy-wrapped in six-inch ace bandages from the sole of my foot to mid-thigh. After we arrived at the casino, we walked around looking for the showroom.

All at once, my friend started laughing hysterically. She pointed to my foot. The ace bandage had unraveled, and I was trailing a five-foot section of it. I laughed, too, and headed for the bathroom to wind myself up again. Before the performance, I waved at The Roadie as he bustled about. The show was quite entertaining.

Liaisons do remind me a bit of my relationship with my dogs. When I'm with them, they often have my undivided attention. When I'm away during the day, I rarely think about them. They have their water and food out all the time and a doggie door. I walk them when I feel like it.

I went back up to my cabin during the summer and saw The Roadie when I needed to return to Scottsdale about once a month. I never asked him up to the cabin. When the anecdotes dried up, and we didn't have any new shared experiences, there was nothing new on the menu. The Roadie stopped texting as often and I didn't mind.

Lesson learned: Liaisons don't go deeper. They stay the same until both people drift away.

Chapter Twenty-Two

The Train Man Stops at My Station Again

The next summer, the Train Man contacted me, claiming I'd stopped returning his calls. I didn't remember it that way.

On our first date the second summer of our romance, he took me to his daughter's thirtieth birthday party at Granny's Closet restaurant in Flagstaff, and I met two of his kids and three grandchildren. This sent me the message that he wanted to continue our relationship, since I was important enough to introduce to his family.

For our next date, I agreed to go out for East Indian food. I liked this guy a lot, if I was willing to do that. I hadn't eaten Indian food in a while because I don't like curry or saffron. We had chicken Tandoori, naan, and a bowl of pureed spinach with squares of homemade cheese. I was a little put off by the bright red color of the chicken. The spinach dish was tasty, but not appetizing to look at. The meal was okay, but it didn't spark a love for Indian food. I'd take a pizza any time.

An interesting aspect of the relationship with The Train Man was his work schedule. It mutated and made it impossible to plan anything ahead of time unless he took vacation days. He drove the train to Needles, stayed overnight, and then came back a day or two later. This gave me the freedom to live my life as I pleased, but it was frustrating. *Can't have everything.*

Las Vegas

He planned a few days in Las Vegas. We took my car because it's a hybrid and got excellent gas mileage. We stopped in Seligman, and ate at a fantastic German restaurant, Westside Lilo's Café.

When we reached Vegas, we headed straight to the strip and took in a floor show while we sipped margaritas. Then we played blackjack in the Paris casino. He was a serious gambler while I was a dabbler, so when I got bored, I wandered around and people-watched.

He had procured tickets to a rock 'n roll revue show which was fun. Then it was off to our hotel on Fremont Street. After checking in, we dined on inexpensive shrimp cocktails. We did the Fremont Street Experience—a light and musical show. That night, many bands performed playing eighties music. It was the first time I saw lots of guys dancing by themselves in front of the bands.

By midnight, I was tired. I returned to the hotel room while Train Man gambled. He came back around four in the morning and we made love. When he undressed, I realized he was "commando," no underwear. How did I never notice that?

On the way back to Flagstaff, we took Route 66 and stopped at Laughlin, a casino town in Nevada near the Arizona border. We stayed the night, gambling and listening to live music. Then we went to Oatman, a former Arizona mining town that features wild donkeys roaming the streets, some artisans, and a make-believe shoot-out. I thoroughly enjoyed myself and was surprised how well we got along 24/7.

Weekend in Rocky Point

On one of our many dates to see The Monday Night Blues Band in Flagstaff, I had introduced my friend D to his friend J. On the spur of the moment that fall, D, J, Train Man and I traveled to Rocky Point, Mexico. I'm not an impulsive person and this felt like so much fun, letting go and allowing the Train Man to plan the trip.

I raced down to Scottsdale the day before to get a bathing suit and my passport, which the Train Man insisted I didn't need.

On Saturday morning, the guys picked us up at nine-fifteen. J was driving his Lincoln sedan, which was quite comfortable. As he drove, J told us about how he sometimes saw double, due to his diabetes. D and I glanced at each other with raised eyebrows.

Train Man saw we were worried and took over the driving when we stopped west of Phoenix. Since Train Man had been to Rocky Point many times, he had to stop at his favorite rest places. I sat beside Train Man in the front seat. Between Phoenix and Ajo, it became apparent that the air conditioning didn't reach the back seat. Poor D. It didn't seem to bother J. He regaled us with stories that started out like they were true but ended up as jokes.

We stopped in Why, Arizona to refuel the car and get snacks. Why borders the Tohono O'Odham Reservation and has a tiny convenience store with a casino. While D, J, and I picked out goodies to eat, Train Man played the slots and won sixty dollars.

Mid-afternoon, we arrived at our hotel, Playa Bonita. The guys took care of registering and carrying the bags to the rooms. D and I went to the outside bar that overlooked the Sea of Cortez and ordered frozen margaritas—D had a double, and I had a single. Happy hour arrived, with reduced prices for the margaritas and food, so we ordered more drinks and guacamole. The guys joined us and J shared D's drink. We enjoyed the ambiance.

Train Man, the tour leader, said we were going on a sunset dinner cruise. D and I wanted to change out of our shorts into something nicer. On the way to the dock, Train Man said that *altos* (stop signs) and license plates were optional in Mexico. After that, at every intersection, we chanted the refrain, "Optional."

Onboard *The Intrepid* for our dinner cruise, the DJ's music was too loud until the free margaritas and beer started flowing. I didn't mind the noise after that. The sunset was spectacular. I kept jumping up and taking photos from different angles as the sun descended over the sea.

Passengers danced, including us. J had to hang onto the pole while he was dancing, so Train Man called him a pole dancer. We ate delicious fish tacos and watched the full moon rise like a huge gold coin.

After the cruise, we retrieved the car from the paid parking where a woman had watched over it. Train Man drove us downtown. He had trouble parking the car and it ended up three feet from the curb. Guess I wasn't the only who felt our free drinks.

We walked to Flavio's, one of Train Man's favorite haunts, and secured a table overlooking the sea. Train Man had more Tecate light and the rest of us shared a pitcher of frozen strawberry margaritas. This sweet concoction contained almost no alcohol, so we sobered up. The Oysters Rockefeller that Train Man ordered were scrumptious. Three different groups of mariachis serenaded us when the singer took his break.

The next morning, we eschewed the buffet at the hotel for Max's, a restaurant started by a guy from Brooklyn. I enjoyed a breakfast of bagels, lox, cream cheese, and capers. Then headed downtown to shop. Train Man helped D barter for a wallet and a red purse. Then he sat on a bench eating some dried fruit he bought from a vendor, while we shopped some more. We stopped for piña coladas served in coconut shells. I bought a pair of earrings and was pleased when the vendor told me I looked like a Mexican movie star in them.

Back at the hotel, Train Man announced it was time for a banana boat ride, an inflatable with two bananas on each side and a small platform in between. The bananas have hand holds, and the boats seat up to eight people. A motor boat pulls the inflatable through the water.

We had the whole banana to ourselves, with Train Man and me up front. I was wearing a long tee shirt over my bathing suit and couldn't get a grip on the plastic seat. I fell over but was laughing too hard to say anything.

J yelled out, "Annie needs help." The boatman eased up on the accelerator, and I righted myself. We took off again at high speed, and I landed in the middle again. With help, I climbed up on the banana again and finished the wild ride.

At the patio of the hotel, I ordered a double frozen margarita to steady my nerves. J and D each decided they needed a nap. After a while Train Man and I took another banana boat ride. This time I took off my tee shirt and stayed upright because my swimsuit bottom hugged the plastic of the banana boat. And the best part? We saw dolphins. The driver stopped the boat within ten feet of them. I'll never forget the glory of seeing them so close.

That night we listened to Rigo, a great singer in the hotel bar, and watched the sun set. Train Man knew Rigo from previous visits and he came over to talk to us. Train Man bought us copies of Rigo's CD..

After dancing cheek-to cheek, we strolled on the beach, looking at the stars and listening to the quiet lapping of the waves. So romantic.

The next morning, as we headed back to the US border, we encountered a hiccup. We American citizens were fine, even without Train Man's passport. Since J was a Canadian citizen and didn't have his passport, the border patrol officer took him out of the car and did some checking. After ten tense minutes, J was back in the car and good to go.

What a wonderful lost weekend at Rocky Point, Mexico. I memorialized the trip with a photo book, which I copied and gave to Train Man, D, and J.

The Train Man and I were getting along so well, I agreed to take an Alaskan cruise with him in May. He wanted the points on his American Express card, so I gave him a check for the cruise. We coordinated our air flights, but I bought my own ticket.

I wrote about the Train Man on my blog (www.thesinglesenior.wordpress.com) in December and received a surprise comment. The woman stated that she thought we were going out with the same man. What?

This disconcerted me for two reasons. One, the Train Man and I hadn't agreed on an exclusive relationship, but I chose to remain ignorant about anyone else he was dating. I had fooled myself into thinking we were exclusive, so I didn't require a condom when we had sex.

Secondly, I'd love to think my blog was so popular anyone would stumble on it. Unfortunately, that's not true, so how did she get to my blog? When I wrote back, the woman said she saw the book of photos I'd made of our Rocky Point trip in the waiting room of J's auto-repair business and Googled me. She wrote on and on about how she'd been to Train Man's house and thought he was going to marry her. I stopped the conversation and called J. He stammered a bit but confirmed that the Train Man saw other women. Okay, I thought. I asked if any were serious girlfriends, and he said no.

The Train Man invited me to go to Rocky Point again in January. He invited his grown son to go with us without asking me, which was a little weird. Why did we have to take my car? I wasn't sure, except it's a Honda Civic Hybrid and got great mileage.

The four-and-a-half hour ride from Phoenix to Rocky Point passed quickly as I conversed with Train Man's son. We stopped at all the same places on the way to Mexico, then checked into the hotel and played the day away.

When we returned to our room that evening, we were both eager to make love. We hugged and kissed, then—probably not the best timing on my part—I summoned the courage to tell him I knew about the other woman, but that it didn't bother me. The only request I made was that he begin using a condom for both of our safety. Looking back, I wish I had told him how I found out about the other woman, and that she had said they were getting married.

He turned away from me and then glanced back with a cold stare. He said he was allergic to latex. I said we could probably find a substitute the next day.

That started the Silent Treatment. He wouldn't talk to me unless we were with his son. At those times, while horseback riding, listening to music, and eating meals, he was quite amiable. As soon as we were alone, he clammed up. A mixture of anger and confusion made me miserable.

It was a long weekend. I was glad I'd brought my Kindle because I had trouble sleeping. When we returned to the place where he'd parked his car in Phoenix, I asked if our cruise should be canceled. He refused to answer.

At home, two mornings later, I checked my reservation for the cruise but couldn't find it, so I called the cruise line. He'd canceled for both of us. I left a curt message on his phone that I expected a check for the money I'd given him. Then I called up the airline, not known for being easy to deal with, to cancel my reservations. The clerk was unbelievably nice when I told her the circumstances. She said I never responded to an email they'd sent, changing the time of the flight for half an hour later. If I wouldn't accept the change, she could refund all my money.

I received an envelope from the Train Man the next day with a check. No note. Never heard from him again. I didn't get it. He seemed like such a great guy. He had the seal of approval from my friends, but he fooled us all. I would never have thought him capable of such a cold streak. How could I have discerned this?

Lesson learned: I'm not sure.

Chapter Twenty-Three
Mr. Strike Out

When I checked my mail on the Plenty Of Fish dating site, I had a missive from a fellow whose picture looked familiar. In his email he reminded me that we had met for one date several years ago and shared passionate kisses on my patio. Oh yeah, I'd had high hopes then, but he called off the relationship before it started because he was making another try with his ex-girlfriend. Available again, he wanted to reconnect. The guy had been honest with me, and the chemistry was alive, so I agreed to meet him for a drink at Humble Pie. Question: Do the staff at that restaurant realize I meet first dates there?

Mr. Strike Out was already at a table in the outdoor area when I arrived. Shorter than I remembered—barely taller than me—he was otherwise attractive. He had styled black hair sprinkled with distinguished gray along the temples, wore preppy-style clothes, and his face reminded me of a Roman statue. We drank wine and then shared a salad and a pizza. I suggested the clam topping, but he said he hated squishy food like that.

I listened to his tales of woe. Mr. Strike Out had moved to Pennsylvania for a job that turned out not as advertised. He didn't like the company or the people he worked with, so he quit and came back to Phoenix. Then he had recently found a job and was in the training class when he was told he didn't fit in with their work culture and was abruptly fired. The truly boring instructor had made snide remarks to him. When he pressed for a reason for the firing, management said that he was surfing the net during class, a direct violation of a rule that had been presented. Strike Out argued that he hadn't seen that slide and neither had any of the other trainees.

But you were off task many times and they caught you. I didn't say anything aloud.

Now his plan was to take classes to learn how to construct websites. He was already getting his social security, and unemployment benefit would be another two thousand a month since he had worked in Pennsylvania, where the benefits were much better.

I had only a few rules for the men I date. They had to be employed or financially self-sufficient, and they couldn't be crazy. It sounded like he was okay in the money department.

We shared a kiss when he walked me out to my car. It was hot. I wanted to go out with him again.

Mr. Strike Out called a few days later and explained that his unemployment debit card hadn't arrived yet. He'd like to see me but couldn't offer to pay. My women's lib views surfaced, and I said we could take turns paying for the dates. Since he paid for the last one, I'd treat him to dinner at Frank and Lupe's.

The day of the date had been a tough one since I was dealing with an errant son, and I needed to escape. At dinner, I ordered a pitcher of margaritas and drank at least three glasses—too much for me. I was tipsy when it was time to leave and wasn't going to drive myself home, so he offered to take me home.

Chatting in my living room led to kissing, passionate but reserved in that his hands did not wander. After I sobered up, he drove me back to the restaurant so I could retrieve my car.

Christmas was a hard time of year for me. When I was married, both of my husbands celebrated Christmas. When I got divorced, I was alone. The kids were with their dads. So, when this fellow called and invited me to go out for Chinese food on Christmas

Eve, I readily accepted. Mr. Strike Out said he had a coupon for twenty-five dollars, but could I spot the rest if the tab went over that? I was beginning to feel uncomfortable with his lack of finances, but I agreed.

We went to The Golden Buddha at the Chinese Cultural Center. When he presented the coupon to the host, he apologized and said the restaurant's contract with the coupon's website had ended November first. My date explained that he had just bought the restaurant coupons the day before on a deal from *Good Morning America*. The host sympathized, pointing to a sign on the front door and explained that at least fifty people had come in with the same deal.

He was nonplussed, so I hurriedly agreed to pay for the meal to save his dignity. At least he didn't make a fuss to the host or rail about it during dinner. Instead I was treated to his tales of woe about how his adult daughters didn't care to spend time with him.

Alarms went off in my head. Why was he estranged from his daughters? Didn't he have any friends to spend the evening with? The guy was seriously depressed. At least the General Tso chicken and the beef chow fun were delicious and not too expensive.

When we arrived at my house, I invited him in for courtesy's sake. Thank goodness he declined. We made a date for New Year's

Eve to attend a party at a hotel. When I closed the door behind me, I kicked myself for agreeing to go out with him again. I am too much of an optimist, always expecting things will get better.

I didn't hear a word from him and anxiety settled in. Should I get an outfit ready for a party? As New Year's approached, he didn't call. I hoped I was off the hook, but annoyed that he was so rude as to not communicate with me. On December thirtieth, I finally received a voice mail from him, saying that we were still on for the party, but he didn't have enough money for dinner beforehand. He also had to rethink his life as he was denied unemployment and he couldn't live on his social security, so he would probably have to take an IT job out of state.

I thought long and hard before returning his call. I told him that I didn't want to be a further worry and burden for him, and perhaps it would be better if he called me after he got his life together. He thanked me for understanding. I won't hear from him again, but two strikes and you're out. First time, back with an ex-girlfriend. Second time, financial and family problems.

Whew. Dodged another one.

I spent a fabulous New Year's Eve with Sparky, my dog, watching the ball drop at ten and going to sleep. Sparky was the perfect date. He gave me unconditional love, listened intently, and wasn't burdened with financial woes or ex-girlfriends.

Lesson learned: Do not go out with a Christian man on Christmas Eve.

Chapter Twenty-Four
More First Dates

First dates were a category unto themselves. Generally, men didn't stop talking on the first and second dates. They share more information about themselves than in the next six months. I've stopped looking for the "initial attraction," or chemistry. That just meant it might be a torrid affair that fizzled out quickly. Of course, that'd be okay, too. As I've stated, I have two criteria for guys I date: They must be self-supporting and not crazy—a surprisingly low bar.

One guy claimed to be five feet nine inches tall—a lot of guys lie about their height. I met him in a bar/restaurant at Desert Ridge. I saw immediately that he was truthful about his height, a good start. Clean shaven, he wore an ironed shirt. He was physically fit, which matched his statements about frequenting the gym most days and taking spin classes twice a week.

I ordered a Michelob Ultra and he seconded it. Good, not a heavy drinker. As I expected, he did most of the talking. He expounded on his careers—he was a Hershey's salesman, about the places he'd lived, his new house, his children, and the ex-wife. He also told jokes, and I laughed a lot. That's a good thing. Anyone who can get me giggling racks up extra points.

When it came time to reorder drinks, I asked for a diet Coke. He dittoed that. Another good sign. We ate off the half-priced appetizer menu. Good food and plenty of it. We talked for about two and a half hours, and he paid the tab. In former dating forays, the date and I have split the bills, but I'm on a tight budget these days, so let chivalry do its thing. We both voiced that we'd sign on for another date. No specific plans were made.

A funny joke from him arrived the next day in my email. I wrote back that I liked the joke. Haven't heard from him since. Guess he met someone who piqued his interest more. Another damned rejection. And I thought this date had promise.

Another date was at Starbuck's with a software engineer. He arrived first and made no effort to get my drink, so I ordered and paid for my own iced tea.

He told me all about his career and his Gestalt work with a therapist. The engineer was a logical guy who was in touch with his feelings. Sounded good. He also said I was better looking than my pictures on the website. Flattery helped. On his profile, he listed himself as "separated," but he didn't address it, so I did. He'd been separated for three years and the ex lived in the state of Washington.

Okay, but why wasn't he divorced?

When he asked about adventures I'd had, I told him about teaching in China for ten weeks. He said that he'd spent a week at a nudist resort in Florida. In fact, Mr. Gestalt had a voucher for a week at a luxury nudist resort in Florida and was looking for someone to take.

OMG! That would be my worst nightmare. I remember when a friend was turning thirty, and the surprise party for her was supposed to include a hot tub of pasta in which we would all hang out. I worried about that for weeks because I knew her crowd did hot tubs in the nude. Luckily, the hot tub conveniently broke, and the party took a more conventional route. I gently confessed that I didn't have a good enough body image to participate in nudist activities. He accepted that but said that great bodies weren't the point. Hmmm. I'd said poor body image, not bad body.

Mr. Nudist asked if I would go out with him again. When he asked what kind of date I preferred, I immediately said my favorite, listening to live music. He had been to the Rhythm Room and said he'd made a date for Saturday night but was willing to cancel it. That bothered me. I was not going to be the cause of a cancelled date. We arranged to go dancing on Sunday night.

Me and the Nudist?

The date never happened. He cancelled. He must have found someone who took him up on his offer.

I went on a date with a guy who asked why people in the arts were usually politically liberal. The question intrigued me. I suggested we meet to discuss it, assuming he was also a liberal. We spoke on the phone several times and he made me laugh. Another good sign. I agreed to meet him for lunch against one of my rules of a first date: never commit for more than a drink or iced tea. That way, if the guy is unsuitable for a variety of reasons, it's easy to leave whenever I want.

He suggested Thai food. When I suggested a place that was reasonably priced, he rejected it as mediocre. Why did I always have to come up with the place to meet? I then suggested Malee's On Main in downtown Scottsdale. I'd never been there, but it's always on a list of the valley's best restaurants.

He asked what I would be wearing. I told him he would recognize me because I looked just like the picture on my profile. I recognized him right away, waiting for me outside the restaurant. Miracle. We both had posted photos that were recent. The host seated us at a window table. The place was nearly empty, although it filled as we ate. I was relieved that the lunch prices were within my price range as I was going to offer to pay my share.

We settled in and told each other some of our life stories. He was a bit older than me, but economically secure. He still sold insurance part-time to Medicare-eligible people.

After I stated my opinions, he revealed himself to be a conservative, not a liberal. He chose to discuss religion, politics, and abortion, not usual topics for a first meeting. Our opinions were opposites. It never degenerated into an argument because he was the type of person who thought others were entitled to their wrong opinions. And he told me in no uncertain terms how wrong I was. I sat and seethed, not wanting to make a scene. Although both of us said we'd do another date, he was toast. It's hard to say "no" in person and easier to just not communicate further.

A few months later, I saw the movie *Magic Mike XXL*, and it reminded me how much I liked male companionship. I'd gone through a dry spell of dating. This time I decided to join a mature dating site, Our Time. It cost some money and I anted up. I put in a minimal profile as most people judge by your picture. I chose a recent photo.

I received a lot of emails. Most of the men who responded described themselves as politically conservative. I have friends who have engaged me in discussions where I had to defend Obamacare. That's not how I wanted to spend a date, so. I sent those fellows an email saying, "I am not currently dating men with conservative political views."

I went back to the free site, Plenty of Fish, and found more guys with conservative views, but I also found three likely candidates and made meet-up dates with them.

The first date was at Houston's, a restaurant near my house. We had two beers apiece and talked for a few hours. He was much better looking in person as he had a terrible selfie on the website. We didn't have much in common, but he told great stories about his family, there was some chemistry, and he didn't ask me to pay. Unfortunately, I never heard from him again. Another rejection. It's more like a sting now, rather than a stab to my ego.

I met another date at Z Tejas. I got caught in a sudden downpour without an umbrella. I arrived on time but plastered with rain—not a great first impression. We sat at a table and ordered appetizers.

When I ordered a beer, he gaped and declared that he never drank when he had to drive. I didn't change my order as I planned to have only one.

He told me about the problems he was having with his troubled son. I could certainly empathize as I also had a struggling son, so I understood his dilemma and conflicting feelings.

The chemistry was inert between us, and while I empathized with his family problems, I didn't need another friend with serious issues. He texted me a few times for advice on his teenager and I obliged. We didn't have a second date.

I made a date with a fellow and agreed to meet at a Starbuck's in the east valley, about twenty miles from my home because I had other errands on that end of town.

I arrived a few minutes before nine, the appointed time, and ordered a large iced tea and a breakfast sandwich. I didn't wait to eat my sandwich because I wanted to have time to check in the bathroom mirror in case some of the spinach caught in my teeth.

I had neglected to get his phone number, but I emailed him on the POF dating site exactly where the Starbuck was. At nine-thirty I emailed him again. I could see he was on the site at that time, and that burned me. Why was he flirting with other women when he already had a date with wonderful me? My email said, "Guess you're not interested. Sorry I wasted a trip."

An hour later I received an email from him apologizing and explaining that he had it on his calendar for ten o'clock. I, in fact, have done a similar thing to my hairdresser. Neglecting to check my calendar, sure that my appointment is for two, I receive a phone call from her that it was at one. The calendar backs her up. I decided to give him another chance, but he never contacted me again.

Lesson learned: Get the man's telephone number so he can be called if there's a snafu.

Chapter Twenty-Five
Mr. Hot Stuff

I met Mr. Hot Stuff in Munds Park through the website POF. Our first date was a beer at The Pinewood Restaurant. We closed the place up at nine. I felt instant chemistry. He seemed like a decent guy, too.

He invited me to his house for dinner the next night. I was a bit wary, but this is Munds Park, with fewer than three thousand people during the summer. He lived only a mile from my place.

We talked and laughed and kissed passionately on his couch.

Our next date was dinner at my place. I made my famous Machaca chicken quesadillas and served frozen margaritas. Both of us got tipsy and we made out again. My body was aching for his, but we didn't have sex.

We drove to Flagstaff to listen to my favorite local band, The Mother Road Trio, the next time we went out. I nearly swooned when he held me tightly as we slow-danced. Would the romance last a week or two or even the summer or maybe more? I decided to enjoy it as it came.

We tried staying at my house for the night, but my dogs were jealous of Mr. Hot Stuff and kept us up most the night. After that, I stayed at his place. People brag about how smart their dogs are. Mine aren't and I like it that way. I would stay at Mr. Hot Stuff's house until four in the morning, go home, tell the dogs it was the last pee of the night and take them outside. I gave them their nightly treats and we went to bed for a few hours. They bought it every time.

Mr. Hot Stuff even accompanied my granddaughters and me when we went to Cliff Castle Casino to bowl and have lunch. Things were going well.

In September, he told me he was going to Memphis for a month to visit friends. We texted occasionally, much less than we had during the summer. When he returned, I tried to arrange a date, but he texted me that he was trying to get back with his second ex-wife, and she had returned with him from Memphis.

Anger again. Why can't men be honest with me? If he'd told me that he was going to Memphis to get back with the ex-wife, I would have accepted the end of a summer romance.

Immediately after I graduated from college, I got married and moved to

Cleveland, Ohio. We lived in an efficiency apartment and slept on a convertible couch. When we stepped up to a one-bedroom apartment, we bought a double bed. I slept in that double bed until I moved to a new house with husband number two, who was six foot three inches tall. He bought a queen-sized bed. When the marriage ended twelve years later, he took the bed with him and I went back to the double bed that had a head and footboard.

I had a queen-sized bed at my cabin, and it seemed enormous. My dog Louie slept in the place where someone else's head would be. Sparky usually stayed on the floor. I'd been thinking about buying a new bed for my condo in Scottsdale as the mattress was fourteen years old, minus the seven months a year when I spend the summer in Munds Park.

Enter Mr. Hot Stuff. He's six foot six inches. No way would he fit in my double bed. But when we broke up after Labor Day, I put the idea of a new bed on hold.

When I mentioned the bed quandary to a good friend she said, "Having a double bed advertises that you're not interested in a relationship."

After much cogitating, I decided to get the queen-sized bed.

I headed to downtown Phoenix to the Tuft and Needle store to try out their mattresses. Question: Why is the company called Tuft and Needle when the mattress contains two kinds of foam with no sewing or tufting?

Several "bedrooms" had doors so shoppers could go into one and try out the mattress in private. The first bed seemed a bit firm for me. When I spoke with a salesperson, she said that the mattress would conform to my body within two weeks. And I had one hundred days to decide if I liked it. If I didn't, I'd let them know, they'd refund my money, and I'd donate the mattress to a charity. Since the company's headquarters was in Phoenix, the mattress could be delivered the next day. It came vacuum-packed in a box. It seemed a fool-proof plan, so I bought a queen-sized one.

Once home, I immediately ordered a box spring for a hundred twenty dollars on Amazon. Since I have Prime, the shipping was free. I had bought my youngest son a bed last February, and he'd never used the bedframe, so I picked that up from his place.

The Tuft and Needle mattress didn't need a frame or box spring, but I wanted the bed high enough so I wouldn't have to tax my knees when I climbed in and out of bed.

Although there's nothing wrong with my knees, I was thinking forward.

Imagine my surprise when the box spring came in a tall and skinny box. Hmm. It required assembly. I reread the order and sure enough, it read, "some assembly required." Shoot. As I've said before, mechanical ability is not one of them.

Fast forward to Thanksgiving. Mr. Hot Stuff texted me, "Happy Thanksgiving." That started a dialogue that ended with him coming down to visit for a day. It hadn't worked out with the ex-wife, so I thought we were back on. I asked Mr. Hot Stuff to put the bed together. He was happy to leave the cold of Munds Park and help me out.

I had started my new job, so I worked in my office while he wrestled with the bed. I had a bad cold and was existing on hot tea with lemon and honey. He put the frame together in no time. When he opened the carton for the box spring, he called me into the bedroom to see sixty steel pieces.

After another cup of hot tea, he started the task of putting it together. Meanwhile, I retreated to my office. After an hour, I ventured into the bedroom to check on his progress. Although sweating up a storm, he was excited because he'd figured it out.

"I'm building a steel box with steel slats. There's a zippered cover that surrounds it," he said.

"Are you ready for a break?"

"I'll take a break and a glass of water, but I want to finish the box spring before we have lunch."

He worked for another half an hour and then called me in to help him put on the cover.

"This is a steel box. It's never going to wear out."

"Hmm, great," I answered. Did any box springs ever wear out?

We struggled, but finally managed to encase the steel box with the fabric and zip it up. When would I ever need to wash a box-spring cover?

After lunch, we attended the basketball game of a friend of mine—the coach of a freshman girls' team. Neither team played well, but our team lost.

Upon returning home, Mr. Hot Stuff opened the box and we both tugged out the mattress, then positioned it on the box spring. The vacuum-packed mattress was only two inches thick, but as soon as he cut the packaging, it morphed to eight inches thick immediately.

We went to bed that night on the new mattress, but we just slept together. No kissing, no hugging, no fooling around. Our relationship had gone from lovers to friends without benefits.

One time when he visited, we went to a matinee to see *Rogue One, A Star Wars Story*. It was playing at Shea 14, an older theater not too far from my home in Scottsdale. I'm not a huge sci-fi fan, but I do love *Star Wars*.

Friends always gave me the Harkins shirt and loyalty cup for Hanukkah, so I got a free popcorn and $1.50 soda refill. I upgraded to a large popcorn for a dollar so I could share with Mr. Hot Stuff and bought him a loyalty cup filled with soda. It was already dark in the theater when we chose our seats. He sat on the aisle to accommodate his long legs.

Of course, about three-quarters of the way through the movie, I had to go to the bathroom. I quickly exited, visited the ladies' room and raced back to my seat since I didn't want to miss the action.

As the credits were rolling, I said, "Since this is a prequel, we know how it ends."

"Yes, no mystery there," an unfamiliar voice answered.

My eyes darted left to see a nearly bald man, Mr. Hot Stuff's follicle situation, but it wasn't Mr. Hot Stuff. I blanched and scanned the room. There sat Mr. Hot Stuff with an amused look on his face across the aisle and a row behind me. Laughing hysterically, I slid into the seat next to Mr. Hot Stuff. .

On his way out, the other follically-challenged man stopped at our row. "Just don't tell my wife," he said.

I'm glad he had a sense of humor. I had nearly gained my composure when the people across the aisle stood and said, "We got it all on video on our phone."

This set off more belly laughs.

As we exited the theater, Mr. Hot Stuff said between chortles, "I was worried. I thought either you hated the movie or I'd come out to find ambulances."

That evening, every time one of us mentioned the incident, another round of laughter burst forth. It did me a world of good and didn't cost as much as a therapist.

Mr. Hot Stuff took a temporary contract job for February and March with the same company I worked for. He was supposed to work in northern Arizona, but they needed help in the Phoenix area. He asked if he could stay with me during the week. I agreed.

We got along well. He made dinner most days, putting the ingredients in the Crock-Pot before we left for work. In the evenings we discussed how the day had gone. We slept in the same bed, but had no sex.

Every day I had to wrestle three fifty-pound cases in and out of my car. Then I hoisted them onto tables and counters to charge the ten tablets in each case. Mr. Hot Stuff figured out how to bundle the cords so it was easy to plug and unplug the tablets. He started out helping me load and unload the cases, but it hurt his back. I must have been in better shape because it didn't hurt me. All those Saturdays at the gym were worth it.

We talked about our relationship, and he told me he was thinking about moving back to Fresno, where his children and grandchildren resided. I certainly understood. I tried to make him realize that "just for the moment" was fine with me, but he said he didn't want to hurt me. We still hadn't had sex since the summer.

After the job was completed, he returned to Munds Park and then to Fresno. He did text me happy birthday wishes in the middle of March. After one more text in March and two in April, he never texted me again. Ever the optimist, I thought maybe he was ill. I drove past his house in mid-June and saw him coming out of his house. He was fine.

I texted him the next week and got a response that I was texting the wrong number. Huh? He went from lover to friend to ghost. Friends don't treat friends that way, even without benefits.

Lesson learned: I still don't know how to read men.

Chapter Twenty-Six
Creeped Out and Complimented in the Same Night

I was a huge Phoenix Suns fan, having had season tickets for twenty years, until they passed my price point. One night, the Suns were playing the Miami Heat. I decided to watch it down the block at a sports bar that had great burgers and sweet potato chips. After the game, I planned to catch one set of The Sugar Thieves at the Rhythm Room.

When I got to the bar, the manager pointed to the set he would put the game on, and I chose a table in front of it.

I eat out often by myself, so I wasn't the least self-conscious about it. I ordered a Diet Coke and the blue-cheese burger with the sweet potato chips and settled in to watch the game. Although the Suns did horribly the first quarter, they played good ball the second, and it was a close game. At half-time I treated myself to a brownie sundae—delicious but much too big to finish.

In the middle of the third quarter, a young man wrested my attention from the game.

"Are you sitting alone?"

Surprised, I mumbled, "Yes."

"I don't want to sit at the bar. Would you mind if I joined you?"

That's strange. I peered around the room, and realized it had filled up while I was focused on the game. "Sure."

We chatted, but I had a hard time understanding what he was saying because he was slurring his words. Was he drunk or did he have a speech impediment? When he told the waitress I was his girlfriend, I laughed. He ordered one of their very large glasses of beer. The waitress carded him. That's how young he was.

Mr. Carded did know about basketball and the Suns players—no mean feat, as the famous guys on the team had been traded. He ordered wings. When they came, he stuffed one in his mouth and his eyes bugged out. He finished chomping on it and spewed out the bone.

I asked if it was spicy or hot in temperature. He said the latter. But then he popped another one in his mouth with the same effect. Mr. Carded told the waitress he wanted to pay for my meal. I declined, but he wouldn't take no for an answer. Then he put his hand on my shoulder. I shrugged it off, becoming more uncomfortable by the minute.

He paid the bill and called someone to say where he was and that he was with his girlfriend. It was now the fourth quarter of the game and tied. When he got up without a word to me, taking his beer with him, I saw my opening. I slipped out the patio, ran to my car, locked the doors and left, listening to the end of the game on my radio en route to the Rhythm Room.

The place was packed. I paid the eight-dollar cover and stood to listen to the fine blues music. A young man next to me started chatting. I told him about my encounter at the sports bar, and he said he would pick out a suitable guy for me. Luckily, he was with his girlfriend, so he wasn't coming on to me.

I listened to six or so songs, and then headed for the restroom. On the way, a handsome guy with silver hair stopped me and said, "I love your smile." When I returned to my place, I noticed that the handsome guy was glancing at me every now and then.

When the band played a slow tune, I asked Silver Fox to dance. He readily agreed. We didn't talk much, just exchanged names. At the end of the dance, he hugged me and thanked me for sharing my smile with him. Silver Fox didn't make a move to stand and talk with me, so I returned to my place and enjoyed the rest of the set.

So, I got complimented and creeped out in the same night, got to enjoy a well-played basketball game and listen to soul-enriching music.

Lesson learned: Sometimes a night out alone is better than an average Saturday night at home.

Chapter Twenty-Seven
Mr. GQ

I met a man through the Plenty of Fish dating website, and we connected.
Our first date was supposed to be on a Thursday night at The Vig on 40th Street in Phoenix. The place was so packed that even the parking lot across the street was full. I had noticed The Attic Alehouse on my way, with a half-filled parking lot, so I called him and suggested a different meeting place.

The Attic Alehouse wasn't noisy. My date was on time. He matched his picture from the profile on the dating website, only more handsome. I was a bit starstruck, which was superficial of me.

I named the new man Mr. GQ because he dressed like he walked out of that magazine. Stylish and impeccable with perfectly coifed silver hair, he was my height, but I've lost another inch, according to my Medicare "wellness" exam the past week, so he's at least an inch taller. And he carried some meat on his bones, so I wouldn't crush him.

We exchanged some of our life stories and laughed a lot. That's what made me interested in dating him. I needed lightness and chuckling in my life.

We texted for a few days, and I suggested we go dancing at The Rhythm Room. I love that place. The crowd was generally my age, with a sprinkling of young people to keep the place from being an old fogey's hangout. I drove my own car and met him there.

The Bluesmen Feat with Geo Bowman & Diva Missy played a mix of oldies, including Motown hits. He ordered a Diet Coke and Malibu Rum, while I stuck with Michelob Ultra. I tasted his cocktail and decided it might become my drink of choice.

He said he'd dance whenever I wanted to. Mr. GQ didn't need to down two or three drinks before going on the dance floor, and he danced "free-style" like me. Several couples showed off their moves from lessons, but I felt comfortable dancing with him.

He seemed open and honest, but I've said and written that before and been wrong.

For our third date, we went to the movies to see *I Feel Pretty* with Amy Schumer. It didn't get good reviews, but we laughed and enjoyed ourselves. Afterward, we went back to my house and drank Malibu rum and Diet Cokes. We shared more of our life stories. I told him about the plane crash and mentioned that I would like some support on Mother's Day. He said he was having dinner with his children and their mother, but he would come over afterwards. I appreciated that immensely.

We did more than kissing, but didn't make love. He mentioned toys that former lovers had used. I only owned Mr. Buzzy, a silver-bullet vibrator, so I made a mental note to go to The Castle Superstore, to do some shopping.

In between dates, we texted some mundane matters and other sexually suggestive ones.

As soon as I entered the Castle Superstore in Phoenix at ten one morning, I noticed I was the only customer. The young salesman came right over and asked what I was looking for. I told him I would like a "couples" toy. He led me to a section and showed me the anniversary edition of a set of two objects. He went into detail about how to use both. I was surprised that I wasn't at all embarrassed and agreed to buy it, along with a lotion for Mr. GQ, one for me, and a toy cleaner.

Only when the sale was rung up did I have sticker shock. The anniversary item was 229 dollars, but I figured it was an investment in my sexual future. The salesman must have seen a sucker as soon as I walked in. Of course, I had to try it out that night. I wasn't at all sure I got the mechanics right.

On Mother's Day, Mr. GQ came over. He was incredibly kind and supportive. We used the toys, but they weren't worth the big bucks I spent on them.

The next day I drove up to my home in Munds Park near Flagstaff for the summer. I told Mr. GQ I'd be home in two weeks. Would such a fledgling relationship stand the summer separation? We texted every day. I wouldn't say I thought about him all the time, or I was in love, or even in lust, but I liked him.

When we got together two weeks later, I didn't feel any awkwardness. We went for Chinese food and talked about the trivial and the deep. Later, the sex was good even though I didn't bring out my new toys.

After sex, I asked him, "Are we exclusive?"

He didn't reply. Hmm. We'd had the conversation that if he had sex with anyone else, he would use a condom. He hadn't.

The next morning, I couldn't fix him breakfast as I had no milk for coffee or anything in the refrigerator since I'd cleaned it out when I left for the summer. We went to Randy's, my neighborhood restaurant, for breakfast. Unfortunately, they didn't have my favorite dish there, strawberry shortcake.

He mentioned that he had many errands to do since this was his day off. He needed a battery for one of his hearing aids. I didn't realize he wore them.

"It's long story," he said.

"That's okay, I'm ready to listen."

His tale went back to 1987, in New Jersey, when he was divorced from his first wife. He told me about a woman he'd been seeing off and on for thirty years. She moved out to Phoenix and into his apartment sometime after he separated from his second wife. Her daughter had a drug problem and lived on the streets of Phoenix. He sometimes paid for her to stay at a motel. The shocker was that the mother was living in his house, in her own bedroom as a tenant, paying him rent.

I excused myself to go to the restroom. I sat in a stall, shaking my head. I'd finally found a guy I liked, but he wasn't divorced, and his ex-lover was renting a room in his house. What to do.

When I got back to the table, I told him I'd have to chew on what he'd said.

I went to my hair appointment and stewed for a while. Sure, Mr. GQ deserved points for being honest. I knew I came to any relationship with my own heavy baggage—the death of my daughters in a plane crash and my youngest son who was a recovering addict. But could I handle his baggage?

I mulled it over with a few friends. No one gave me advice that hit the mark. I went to dinner at Goldman's Deli and ordered cheese blintzes, my quintessential comfort food, then decided I would call him and tell him I wanted out.

But I chickened out. I told him we should talk. We agreed to meet at my house after work. I least now I knew why I was never invited to his house.

We hugged when he came through my front door. I still hadn't settled on what I would tell him. We sat on separate loveseats with glasses of water in hand and made small talk before I dove into the matter.

"I was surprised to learn that your ex-lover was living in your home," I said, "but I'm glad you told me."

"She moved in about a week before you and I met," he said. "I thought I'd wait a few weeks to see if we'd continue going out."

"I understand. If you'd told me right away, I probably wouldn't have seen you again."

"She really is my tenant, with a separate bedroom. I let her know when I'm not coming home."

"That's only polite when you have a roommate. When I asked you the other night if we were exclusive, you didn't answer."

"I was surprised," he said. "When we first met, you said you didn't want to get married or live with anyone. And your profile on the dating website made it sound like you were into casual relationships."

That took me aback. Wasn't that what I wanted? "I meant monogamous," I lied.

"Oh."

"Remember I asked that if you had sex with another person, you would wear a condom."

"If I put this penis in any vagina, I will certainly wear a condom. I have blood tests quarterly, and I assume they test for STDs."

"Not unless you ask the doctor to write the order that way."

"Hm. So you're good with casual?" he said, his face unreadable.

"Sure," I said, knowing that I wouldn't make supreme efforts to be in the valley as often.

We hugged when he left, and I felt good about our discussion.

Later, however, I had to question myself. Did I want only casual relationships? That may be what I said, but it wasn't true anymore. I still didn't want to get married or live with anyone because I valued my freedom and independence. However, I had to admit that I did want a committed relationship.

I'm not sure when that changed, but I'm sure of it. I'll continue to have casual relationships until I find someone I want to commit to—someone who feels the same way. That may not happen. Or it may.

Lesson learned: Time may change my purpose in dating.

ChapterTwenty-Eight

The Zookeeper or the Weekend that Wasn't

I met the Zookeeper through Plenty of Fish. Our first date was at a Starbucks. He was not as tall as his profile said, but that was nothing new to me. He had a full head of hair, the face of a youngster, and he was stocky, which I liked. Mr. Zookeeper was younger by eight or so years. He walked with a decided limp.

As we talked, I found out that he was divorced and he was involved in his teenage daughter's life. He was preparing to start a new teaching job at a charter school. He had quit his teaching position at a public school because he said he didn't get along with the principal. I've known some principals who picked out scapegoats and favorites, so I didn't question it.

How would the man be able to endure the rigors of a classroom with such a bum knee? He said he was waiting until the next summer to get his knee replaced. Mr. Zookeeper also stated that he was interested in marriage and/or living with someone. I told him in no uncertain terms that I wasn't, although I was looking for a committed relationship. He was lonely, I could tell.

I nicknamed him The Zookeeper because he worked for many years at a primate reserve in Mesa and at the Phoenix and World Wildlife Zoo. It was a young man's occupation, he said, as it was physically strenuous. He shared some funny stories about his work. He told me he'd gone back to school to become a teacher.

On our third date, we met for dinner at La Piñata, a Mexican restaurant in mid-town Phoenix. I frequented the place when it was on 19th Avenue and Osborn and lived close by.

Unfortunately, the food was terrible the night of our date. It's hard to mess up cheese enchiladas, but they were beyond bland. It was the first day of the school year. He taught third grade, and I thought he'd talk about his class, but he didn't. Mr. Zookeeper is a bright man. We chatted about books, movies, and our lives. I gave him copies of two of my books.

I expected him to ask me back to his house to meet his menagerie: three dogs, a desert tortoise, an African tortoise which will eventually weigh three-hundred-fifty pounds, and assorted snakes. After dinner, we headed to the parking lot, where he gave me a quick peck on the cheek.

We texted the rest of that week, I finally summoned the gumption to tell him about my expectation. He answered that he hadn't asked me to his house because it was a mess, adding he was more like Oscar Madison than Felix Unger of *The Odd Couple*. Hmmm. I'm not a neat freak, but how messy could he be? I texted that I could be in a committed relationship with someone who was messy, but not live with him.

I took a risk and asked him to come up to my cabin for the weekend, hoping that the relationship would go to the next level.

He found a sitter for his critters and agreed to drive up on a Friday afternoon after school. I made dinner—machaca chicken/spinach quesadilla, corn on the cob, and homemade guacamole and chips. I arranged for a housekeeper to clean the house and put sheets on the bed in the second bedroom, not wanting to push him into anything he wasn't comfortable with.

When he arrived, I gave him a hug. I was expecting a kiss to alert me to his intentions, but he didn't deliver one. He came in and sat on the couch. I sat next to him, but he didn't hold my hand or touch me.

I finished making dinner, and I guess he liked it because he ate it up. He didn't offer to help with the dishes or take his plate to the sink. Hm.

After dinner he sat on the couch and I sat on the chair across from him, and we talked. The more he conversed, the more red flags went up. Although he wasn't mobile now, due to a bad knee, I gathered that he led a sedentary life, watching old movies. Mr. Zookeeper had been married three times, not two. He didn't count one of them since it only lasted for one year. He had two children from his first marriage, but he had moved from Oregon to the Phoenix area, so he didn't see them much and was estranged from them. Another red flag joined the others.

I discovered he was a Republican. Although he'd voted for Trump—anyone but Hillary—he no longer supported him. He ranted about how African Americans were racist because ninety-eight percent of them voted for Obama. Uh-oh, another red flag.

I don't remember how the topic came up, but he said that once the pill was in wide use, women became as bad as men. Before that, women lived on a higher plane, but now they were the same dogs as men, sleeping around. Another red flag. I was sure he'd be scandalized when my next book, *Sex and the Single Senior*, was published.

I wanted a committed relationship, but I wasn't willing to settle for someone who wasn't a good partner. He didn't fit with my personal or political views. And I needed someone physically affectionate.

It was getting later and later, but he didn't make any comment about going to bed. Finally at midnight, I managed, "I'm tired."

"Do you want me to sleep in the second bedroom?"

"No, you can sleep with me." I took my dog out for his quick night walk and moved Louie's bed into my bedroom. I gave my dog treats so he would stay in his bed and not get up on mine.

Although I had a silky nightgown, I opted for a thick cotton night shirt. He crawled into bed but kept his distance. He continued to talk while I struggled to stay awake. Finally at one, I said I had to sleep.

"Don't you want to get frisky?" he said.

I declined.

I didn't sleep well. In the morning, I got up and took a shower. When I returned to the bedroom, he wasn't there. He was sitting on the living room couch dressed and on his smartphone. I told him I was taking Louie for a walk and knew he wouldn't accompany me because of his knee. It was six-thirty.

As I walked down the block, I called my best friend since seventh grade, who lives in northern California and explained the situation. I dreaded spending the rest of the weekend with him since I knew there was no chance for a relationship.

First, she said she'd call me when I returned to the cabin, and I could say there was an emergency in Scottsdale and I had to get back to the valley. I could pack up a few things, drive behind him until I lost sight of him, then take the next exit back to Munds Park. But that wouldn't solve the bigger problem, and we both agreed that deception wasn't the way to go. I decided on honesty.

When I got returned to the cabin, he was still on his phone. He'd made coffee but hadn't found the artificial sweetener and hadn't wanted to paw through my cupboard. He also informed me that the coffee was decaf. None of my other guests had noticed that. I made him a cup of strong organic black English tea.

I sat across from him and said, "I took a risk in asking you to come up this weekend. I thought it might take our relationship to another level. The problem is, I don't feel a personal connection with you. I'm not taking about chemistry, but a connection. You're a great guy. On paper we look like we're meant for each other. We're both intelligent, love books and movies, and are into education. It just didn't pan out in person. You're a great catch for someone else."

He was quiet for a moment, then said, "I'll pack up and go as soon as I finish my tea."

I felt bad. I guess he liked me, but it didn't come through. After he left, I moved Louie's bed back to the living room. He'd be sleeping with me tonight.

Lesson learned: Just because someone wants a relationship, it may not be right for me.

Chapter Twenty-Nine
The Trucker

I was still seeing Mr. GQ, but it was casual, a friend with benefits. Why? He'd been separated from his wife for more than eight years but was still married, and he rented a room in his home to his ex-girlfriend. Definitely not someone with whom.to have a full-fledged relationship.

I joined a different dating website, Bumble. Both men and women sign up and put up profiles, but the women are the ones who swipe left or right. If a woman has indicated interest, then the man can message her through the app. I swiped right quite a bit and received a few emails. One intrigued me, and we made a date to meet.

We met at a Starbucks the day after Valentine's Day. He looked mostly like his photo, but better. He limped. He told me he had one knee replaced last fall and was having the other one done April first. We talked for more than an hour. He seemed to be self-supporting and not obviously crazy, so I made a second date with him.

Our second date was for dinner at a Mexican restaurant. I met him there as I'm always careful about letting a new fellow know my last name or where I lived.

During our dinner conversation, he told he'd been an EMT for ten years but switched to driving a long-haul truck because his brother was making much more money doing that. He only stopped driving when the truck had a chemical spill a year ago and he ended up in the hospital. He hadn't been to a doctor in many years. Of course, they found things that needed fixing—his knees, cataracts in both eyes, a pacemaker and a filter for his heart.

Now he drove for Lyft temporarily to pay off a credit card. He worked at least nine hours every day. A good work ethic, but he probably hadn't planned for retirement.

Like Mr. Zookeeper, he was a lonely guy, so I immediately put up parameters. I still wasn't interested in getting married or living with someone. Since he was a considerate fellow, he took my boundaries seriously. He was concerned if he was crowding me or asking to see me too much.

Another Republican, but he was a moderate one. Many discussions on current events highlighted our differences, but always with respect for each other's opinion. I got him reading *The New York Times*, so he might change his point of view.

I liked his company. Easy to be around, The Trucker didn't need to be entertained. He didn't take himself too seriously and shared funny anecdotes about his past. And he liked to listen to live music and danced as best he could, given the bad knee.

When I decided it was time to have sex, I texted Mr. GQ that now we would be friends without benefits. I would let him know how things went.

The Trucker was a considerate lover, but had the same performance problems as most men his age. But his attitude was different. He didn't seem to see it as a test of his masculinity. He satisfied me. He said he was fine about sex.

And he was a good sport. The Trucker wore suspenders so I bought him St. Patrick's Day suspenders and a matching bow tie. He wore them on my birthday when we went to a spring-training game and to The Dirty Dogg Saloon to hear Lane Change. However, he didn't buy me a card or gift. Hm.

He got along with my new dogs, which slept in a crate at night. When I'm alone, they happily go into their crate and are silent. However, when The Trucker slept over, they made noise. One of them whined intermittently.

I got the idea to buy marrow bones, cook them before bedtime, and give them to the dogs when they went into their crates. My plan didn't work out since their gnawing was as loud as their whining.

Was he a candidate for a committed relationship? I thought so at first, being the overly optimistic person I am, but after five weeks, I wasn't sure. He said communication was the key to a relationship, but he failed to answer my texts or phone calls. He said he wasn't good with the phone.

His knee was postponed. He was going to go to rehab afterwards for two weeks, but now he was thinking about recuperating at home. I made it clear I'm not up to nursing.

I organized a fundraising party for Global Volunteers, figuring that would be a non-stressful way for him to meet my friends. We had a date for the night before the party, but he called to cancel because he was sick. He never showed up the next day or called to say he couldn't come to the party.

I reflected on this. Other friends couldn't come because they were sick, and each of them called me. Shouldn't a lover be as considerate as a friend?

Lesson learned: A man's behavior for the first two weeks are not indicative of how he'll treat you going forward.

Chapter Thirty
Conclusions

Some men would jump at the chance to have a relationship with me. Lonely guys. Men who haven't planned for retirement. Those barely making it financially.

My sister, a very wise woman, once told me that the men who have the emotional qualities women want—compassion and sensitivity—don't do well financially in their careers, probably because of those qualities. And the men who are financially secure have qualities women don't want—controlling personalities, aggression, and insensitivity. Therein lies the conundrum. How much does money count?

I would like a committed relationship; however, I choose not to be a nurse or a purse. Men my age have health problems as do most of the women. I don't mind if a fellow doesn't have oodles of money, but it's tough if they're just eking by. I don't have enough money to pay for both of our traveling and entertainment expenses.

My life is full and rich with friends and family. Why do I bother to date? I like sex with more than one person, and I like to be part of a couple.

It's like the lottery. You can't win if you don't play. I don't have high hopes that I'll find someone, but if I stop trying, I definitely won't find anyone. So I buy one more ticket. And then another.

Made in the USA
San Bernardino, CA
25 January 2020